Loyalty a

Those Who
PRETEND

DAG HEWARD-MILLS

Parchment House

THOSE WHO PRETEND

Copyright © 2011 Dag Heward-Mills

First published 2011 by Parchment House
16th Printing 2019

[77]Find out more about Dag Heward-Mills at:
Healing Jesus Campaign
Write to: evangelist@daghewardmills.org
Website: www.daghewardmills.org
Facebook: Dag Heward-Mills
Twitter: @EvangelistDag

ISBN : 978-9988-8572-2-6

Contents

1. The Spirit of A Pretender.. 1

2. How to See Through Disloyal Pretenders...................... 12

3. Intimidation and Disloyalty.. 41

4. How Intimidation Can Stop You from Preaching 56

5. Why You Should Not Be Intimidated 61

6. Seven Things You Must Know about Confusion........... 64

7. What is Familiarity?... 74

8. Four Groups that Are Prone to Familiarity 80

9. Twelve Signs of Familiarity 83

10. Seven Ways to Deal with Familiarity............................. 88

Introduction

There are many things that do not look like disloyalty but are disloyalty. They are the attitudes and behaviour patterns that give rise to treachery and disloyalty. It is important to know about these things because they are often the predecessors of serious leadership crises.

Satan causes confusion in the house of the Lord and uses it to stir up disloyal elements in the church. Many people use pretence, familiarity and their power of intimidation to be disloyal.

CHAPTER 1

The Spirit of a Pretender

1. A pretender carries the spirit of an actor.

2. A pretender has a false and fake personality.

3. A pretender carries the spirit of hypocrisy and disloyalty.

4. A pretender carries the spirit of espionage and the modern-day secret service.

5. A pretender carries the spirit of lies and deception.

6. A pretender carries the spirit of impending destruction. If a pretender is near you, you are in grave danger.

7. A pretender carries the spirit of a murderer because almost all pretenders are destroyers and murderers.

TOP PRETENDERS OF THE BIBLE

1. **DELILAH WAS A PRETENDER. Delilah pretended to love Samson. She comforted him, she relaxed him and made him lie on her knees. In the end it was revealed that she was a liar, a deceiver and a murderer.**

After this it came about that he loved a woman in the valley of Sorek, whose name was Delilah.

The lords of the Philistines came up to her and said to her, "Entice him, and see where his great strength lies and how we may overpower him that we may bind him to afflict him. Then we will each give you eleven hundred pieces of silver."

So Delilah said to Samson, "Please tell me where your great strength is and how you may be bound to afflict you . . . ."

When Delilah saw that he had told her all that was in his heart, she sent and called the lords of the Philistines, saying, "Come up once more, for he has told me all that is in his heart." Then the lords of the Philistines came up to her and brought the money in their hands.

She made him sleep on her knees, and called for a man and had him shave off the seven locks of his hair. Then she began to afflict him, and his strength left him.

She said, "The Philistines are upon you, Samson!" And he awoke from his sleep and said, "I will go out as at other times and shake myself free." But he did not know that the Lord had departed from him (Judges 16:4-6, 18-20; NASB)

2. **JUDAS WAS A PRETENDER. Judas pretended to be a faithful disciple of Jesus Christ. In the end it was revealed that he was a traitor, deceiver and a murderer.**

And Satan entered into Judas who was called Iscariot, belonging to the number of the twelve.

And he went away and discussed with the chief priests and officers how he might betray Him to them.

They were glad and agreed to give him money.

So he consented, and began seeking a good opportunity to betray Him to them apart from the crowd

When He rose from prayer, He came to the disciples and found them sleeping from sorrow, and said to them, "Why are you sleeping? Get up and pray that you may not enter into temptation."

While He was still speaking, behold, a crowd came, and the one called Judas, one of the twelve, was preceding them; and he approached Jesus to kiss Him.

BUT JESUS SAID TO HIM, "JUDAS, ARE YOU BETRAYING THE SON OF MAN WITH A KISS (Luke 22:3-6, 45-48; NASB)

3. **ABSALOM WAS A PRETENDER. Absalom pretended to love his brother when he invited him for a party. In the end, it was revealed that the party was a hoax. His so-called party was just a ploy to kill his brother Amnon.**

Then Absalom her brother said to her, "Has Amnon your brother been with you? But now keep silent, my sister, he is your brother; do not take this matter to heart." So Tamar remained and was desolate in her brother Absalom's house. Now when King David heard of all these matters, he was very angry.

But Absalom did not speak to Amnon either good or bad; for Absalom hated Amnon because he had violated his sister Tamar. Now it came about after two full years that Absalom had sheepshearers in Baal-hazor, which is near Ephraim, and Absalom invited all the king's sons.

Absalom came to the king and said, "Behold now, your servant has sheepshearers; please let the king and his servants go with your servant."

But the king said to Absalom, "No, my son, we should not all go, for we will be burdensome to you." Although he urged him, he would not go, but blessed him.

Then Absalom said, "If not, please let my brother Amnon go with us." And the king said to him, "Why should he go with

3

you?" But when Absalom urged him, he let Amnon and all the king's sons go with him.

Absalom commanded his servants, saying, "See now, when Amnon's heart is merry with wine, and when I say to you, 'Strike Amnon,' then put him to death. Do not fear; have not I myself commanded you? Be courageous and be valiant." The servants of Absalom did to Amnon just as Absalom had commanded. Then all the king's sons arose and each mounted his mule and fled (2 Samuel 13:22-29; NASB)

4. **JAEL WAS A PRETENDER. She deceived Sisera the commander of the Canaanite army. She told him not to be afraid and encouraged him to come in and rest. Jael murdered Sisera brutally by knocking a nail into his head. Few men would even be able to so something as gruesome as that. The soft, comforting, pretending lady was actually a killer. Wow!**

Now SISERA FLED AWAY ON FOOT TO THE TENT OF JAEL THE WIFE OF HEBER the Kenite, for there was peace between Jabin the king of Hazor and the house of Heber the Kenite.

JAEL WENT OUT TO MEET SISERA, AND SAID TO HIM, "TURN ASIDE, MY MASTER, TURN ASIDE TO ME! DO NOT BE AFRAID." And he turned aside to her into the tent, and she covered him with a rug.

He said to her, "Please give me a little water to drink, for I am thirsty." So she opened a bottle of milk and gave him a drink; then she covered him. He said to her, "Stand in the doorway of the tent, and it shall be if anyone comes and inquires of you, and says, 'Is there anyone here? ' that you shall say, 'No.'"

BUT JAEL, HEBER'S WIFE, TOOK A TENT PEG AND SEIZED A HAMMER IN HER HAND, AND WENT SECRETLY TO HIM AND DROVE THE PEG INTO HIS TEMPLE, and it went through into the ground; for he was sound asleep and exhausted. So he died (Judges 4:17-21; NASB)

5. **HUSHAI WAS A PRETENDER. Hushai pretended to be on the side of Absalom. He pretended to give good advice, explaining every point with good reasons. Actually, Hushai was working for king David and had been planted in Absalom's palace to assist king David from the inside.**

It happened as David was coming to the summit, where God was worshiped, that behold, HUSHAI THE ARCHITE met him with his coat torn and dust on his head. David said to him, "If you pass over with me, then you will be a burden to me. But if you return to the city, and say to Absalom, 'I will be your servant, O king; as I have been your father's servant in time past, so I will now be your servant,' then you can thwart the counsel of Ahithophel for me. Are not Zadok and Abiathar the priests with you there? So it shall be that whatever you hear from the king's house, you shall report to Zadok and Abiathar the priests (2 Samuel 15:32-35; NASB)

Now it came about when HUSHAI THE ARCHITE, DAVID'S FRIEND, CAME TO ABSALOM, THAT HUSHAI SAID TO ABSALOM, " LONG LIVE THE KING! LONG LIVE THE KING!" Absalom said to Hushai, "Is this your loyalty to your friend? Why did you not go with your friend?"

Then Hushai said to Absalom, "No! For whom the Lord, this people, and all the men of Israel have chosen, his I will be, and with him I will remain. Besides, whom should I serve? Should I not serve in the presence of his son? As I have served in your father's presence, so I will be in your presence." Then Absalom said to Ahithophel, "Give your advice. What shall we do (2 Samuel 16:16-20; NASB)

6. **THE BROTHERS OF DINAH WERE PRETENDERS. They pretended to accept Shechem's proposal to marry their sister. In actual fact, they were planning the murder of the entire village.**

Now Dinah the daughter of Leah, whom she had borne to Jacob, went out to visit the daughters of the land. When Shechem the son of Hamor the Hivite, the prince of the land, saw her, he took her and lay with her by force.

He was deeply attracted to Dinah the daughter of Jacob, and he loved the girl and spoke tenderly to her. So Shechem spoke to his father Hamor, saying, "Get me this young girl for a wife..."

Shechem also said to her father and to her brothers, "If I find favor in your sight, then I will give whatever you say to me. Ask me ever so much bridal payment and gift, and I will give according as you say to me; but give me the girl in marriage."

BUT JACOB'S SONS ANSWERED SHECHEM AND HIS FATHER HAMOR WITH DECEIT, BECAUSE HE HAD DEFILED DINAH THEIR SISTER.

They said to them, "We cannot do this thing, to give our sister to one who is uncircumcised, for that would be a disgrace to us. Only on this condition will we consent to you: IF YOU WILL BECOME LIKE US, IN THAT EVERY MALE OF YOU BE CIRCUMCISED, THEN WE WILL GIVE OUR DAUGHTERS TO YOU, and we will take your daughters for ourselves, and we will live with you and become one people. But if you will not listen to us to be circumcised, then we will take our daughter and go."

Now their words seemed reasonable to Hamor and Shechem, Hamor's son . . .

All who went out of the gate of his city listened to Hamor and to his son Shechem, and every male was circumcised, all who went out of the gate of his city.

NOW IT CAME ABOUT ON THE THIRD DAY, WHEN THEY WERE IN PAIN, THAT TWO OF JACOB'S SONS, SIMEON AND LEVI, DINAH'S BROTHERS, EACH TOOK HIS SWORD AND CAME UPON THE CITY UNAWARES,

AND KILLED EVERY MALE. They killed Hamor and his son Shechem with the edge of the sword, and took Dinah from Shechem's house, and went forth.

Jacob's sons came upon the slain and looted the city, because they had defiled their sister (Genesis 34:1-4, 11-18, 24-27; NASB).

7. **THE GIBEONITES WERE PRETENDERS. They made as if they were ambassadors who had come from a distant country.**

When the inhabitants of Gibeon heard what Joshua had done to Jericho and to Ai, THEY ALSO ACTED CRAFTILY AND SET OUT AS ENVOYS, AND TOOK WORN- OUT SACKS ON THEIR DONKEYS, AND WINESKINS WORN- OUT AND TORN AND MENDED, and worn-out and patched sandals on their feet, and worn-out clothes on themselves; and all the bread of their provision was dry and had become crumbled.

They went to Joshua to the camp at Gilgal and said to him and to the men of Israel, "We have come from a far country; now therefore, make a covenant with us." The men of Israel said to the Hivites, "Perhaps you are living within our land; how then shall we make a covenant with you?"

But they said to Joshua, "WE ARE YOUR SERVANTS." THEN JOSHUA SAID TO THEM, "WHO ARE YOU AND WHERE DO YOU COME FROM?"

THEY SAID TO HIM, "YOUR SERVANTS HAVE COME FROM A VERY FAR COUNTRY BECAUSE OF THE FAME OF THE LORD YOUR GOD; for we have heard the report of Him and all that He did in Egypt, and all that He did to the two kings of the Amorites who were beyond the Jordan, to Sihon king of Heshbon and to Og king of Bashan who was at Ashtaroth. So our elders and all the inhabitants of our country spoke to us, saying, 'Take provisions in your hand for the journey, and go to meet them and say to them, "We are your servants; now then, make a covenant with us."'

This our bread was warm when we took it for our provisions out of our houses on the day that we left to come to you; but now behold, it is dry and has become crumbled. These wineskins which we filled were new, and behold, they are torn; and these our clothes and our sandals are worn out because of the very long journey."

So the men of Israel took some of their provisions, and did not ask for the counsel of the Lord. Joshua made peace with them and made a covenant with them, to let them live; and the leaders of the congregation swore an oath to them.

IT CAME ABOUT AT THE END OF THREE DAYS AFTER THEY HAD MADE A COVENANT WITH THEM, THAT THEY HEARD THAT THEY WERE NEIGHBORS AND THAT THEY WERE LIVING WITHIN THEIR LAND (Joshua 9:3-16; NASB)

How To Uncover Pretenders

Every leader will face the threat of expert pretenders. Many people are fake actors pretending to be loyal when they are actually your enemies. This book is intended to help you to be aware of the presence of people around you who are constantly pretending to be what they are not. Do not be deceived by the meek-faced people with sheepish grins who appear to admire your every decision. Many of these people are pretending. You must go further and uncover the truth about everyone around you. Watch out for those who do not talk much. They are the ones who have much to hide.

People who do not say anything when they are in your presence, but talk a lot when they are away from you, are good examples of pretenders. Why have one picture when you are near and another picture when you are far?

Samson was in great danger when he relaxed in the presence of a pretending woman. So also will you be in great danger when you relax in the presence of fake followers who do not really like you! Most pretenders are very dangerous people and can lead to the worst kind of crisis in your ministry. You must not be so trusting and accepting of quiet and unknown people. The bible teaches us to prove all things and hold fast to that which is good.

So how are you supposed to uncover and discover pretenders who do not speak their minds? The answer is simple! In the same way that doctors find diseases in your liver, your stomach, your pancreas and other organs. (Mind you, the organs of your body do not speak).

How do doctors find things out? By learning about symptoms and signs that mean a whole lot. Each symptom or sign in the body can lead to an important diagnosis. Similarly, each symptom you notice in a person can lead to the all-important diagnosis that you are dealing with a pretender.

Watch out for the signs and symptoms of a pretender! Like a doctor, believe the signs and symptoms. Do not trust what you see. Look beyond the perfect picture that is presented to you and see the real. You must judge by the actions and not by the presentation. If you allow a pretender to flourish in your midst, you are grooming a potential traitor and murderer. Let's look at a few symptoms and signs that are important in picking up pretenders.

Symptoms and Signs of a Pretender

1. **Notice people who are too quiet!** They could be pretenders. Quiet people are dangerous. All their positive and negative thoughts are stored up within them. They stand still and watch quietly with a lean and hungry look in their eyes. You must develop a proper fear and respect for quiet people!

2. **Notice people who seem to have two temperaments depending on who they are with.** When they are with others they are sanguinous, jovial, chatty and friendly. When they are in your presence, they are quiet, serious, pensive and melancholy. Is it that such a person has two temperaments? Or could it be that they pretend to be something else when they are in your presence?

3. **Notice people who are too perfect and dignified in their presentation of themselves.** Such people have a picture of righteousness, perfection, orderliness and holiness. Often, this is a façade for hidden things and dark secrets. As they look at you through their spectacles you cannot imagine the ignominious activities they can engage in when they feel like it.

4. **Notice people who are too nice.** How can it be that you are always smiling and grinning in every circumstance? Are you never sad? Are you never unhappy? Are you always elated and excited? That cannot be the case.

Watch out for people who seem to have a constant unchanging grin on their faces. Obviously, when negative thoughts come into the minds of such people, there will still be a grin on their faces. You can never tell their wicked thoughts towards you by looking at their faces because they will always be smiling. Indeed, their smiles have become face masks. You need to look a little closer and you will discover the real feelings within these bland-faced individuals.

5. **Notice people who use a lot of make up and take a long time to dress.** Such people have developed the art of pretence. They are experts in covering the real person and presenting a fake and unreal image to any unsuspecting brother. The more naïve, innocent and inexperienced a brother is, the more he is taken in by the presentation of this apparent beauty. Little does he know that ninety percent of the beauty is artificial and took a long time to prepare. New husbands are sometimes shocked when they discover that their pretty bride is twenty

percent of what they thought she was. The hair is false, the nails are false, the eyelashes are false, the teeth are false, the breasts are adjusted, the bottoms are widened and the skin is plastered. When all these things are finally removed and the bad lazy and untrained attitude is also revealed, marriage is ready for a truly stormy journey.

6. **Notice people who are non-committal.** Notice people who do not say either good or bad. It cannot be that you never have anything good to say. And it cannot be that you never have anything bad to say. You must have something in your mind.

Watch out for people who are non-committal. I have noticed that people who say 'I don't belong here or there' actually belong somewhere.

Absalom did not say enough. Absalom said neither good nor bad about his sister being raped. How could that be? Did he not even have a bad comment?

7. **Notice people who have a lot of relationships and affairs.** Such people are used to charming the opposite sex, especially the innocent and inexperienced ones. Men tend to learn what women like and learn how to speak convincingly to them. Women also tend to learn what men like and what works on them. With time, without believing in what you are saying, you learn to speak the words of deception and play the role of a perfect pretender.

CHAPTER 2

How to See Through
Disloyal Pretenders

Let love be without DISSIMULATION. Abhor that
which is evil; cleave to that which is good.

Romans 12:9

To dissimulate is to pretend. Many people conceal their true motives and thoughts through pretence. A dissimulator speaks and acts hypocritically.

Dissimulation is all about disguising and concealing your real feelings by false appearances. Dissimulation or pretending is common amongst Christians today.

Pretending is more common in countries where people tend to show a lot of outward respect. In such cultures, people continue to put up a show of respect even when they don't genuinely feel that way.

This false presentation is the cloak that can also conceal disloyalty. The betrayer's dagger and the disloyal person's intentions are hidden beneath the false front.

A wise leader must learn to recognize words that are smoother than butter and softer than oil but which cover drawn swords (Psalm 55:21).

You must learn not to trust people who cover their dislike for you with deception.

When he speaketh fair, believe him not: for there are seven abominations in his heart. Whose hatred is covered by deceit...

Proverbs 26:25 -26

Eighteen Characteristics of Pretenders

1. Pretenders are angelic. They are too good to be true.

And no marvel; for Satan himself is transformed into AN ANGEL of light.

2 Corinthians 11:14

How can a person be so angelic? How can a person be so nice?

Pretenders are so nice that it is sometimes unbelievable that a person can be so nice and pleasant. Watch out for people who are so nice, so polite so attractive and so pleasant. Can it be that there is someone who always smiles, is never sad and is never upset about anything?

The devil does not just present himself as an angel but as an angel of light. He looks glorious, shining, holy and attractive. What could be better than that? How is it that people are taken in and get married to the ugliest of characters? Ugly characters develop strategies that make them look like angels.

One day, a certain young man came to church with a beautiful young lady. He had found this pretty princess and he wanted to marry her urgently. This girl was an outstanding beauty and she stood out amongst the ladies. Anyone would have been attracted to her.

But you need to watch out when it looks too good to be true and too nice to be real. There is always something not so perfect about these angelic characters. Indeed, all men have eaten of the tree of good and evil. This means that there is always some good in the most evil of men and there is some evil in the best of men.

This young pastor went ahead and married this beautiful princess. In no less than three months I spotted them coming to the church for some special counselling. Indeed, the trouble began soon after marriage. One day, this beautiful bride decided to join another church even though her husband was the pastor of his own church.

He was so embarrassed as his wife went to another church on Sunday morning. The beautiful princess was impossible to control or to lead. One thing led to another until they went through the bitterest of divorces.

In the end, the beautiful princess was not as beautiful as she looked. Always ask yourself, "Can it be as good as it looks? Is there not something else that I don't know?" A prudent man sees the evil ahead but the foolish man sees no evil.

2. **Pretenders have things in their background that are not consistent with their claims.**

> **Then she said to him, "How can you say, 'I love you,' when your heart is not with me? You have deceived me these three times and have not told me where your great strength is."**
> **And it came about when she pressed him daily with her words and urged him, that his soul was annoyed to death.**
>
> **Judges 16:15-16 (NASB)**

Delilah was a Philistine and the Philistines were known enemies of the Israelites. Yet, she seemed to have some extra love for Samson who was the archenemy of the Philistines.

You must not take things for granted. Look carefully into people's background and ask yourself why this person is going out of the way to relate with you.

3. **Pretenders make you sign agreements that you will regret.**

The Gibeonites pretended to be travellers who had come from afar. Through pretence they made Joshua sign an agreement that he would regret. How many marriage agreements have been entered into by false pretences and appearances? A little investigation and a little time would have exposed the pretenders. Joshua would have been saved from a life-changing covenant. If you wait a bit and you investigate a bit you will be helped not to marry the wrong person. It is not easy for pretenders to continue pretending for long periods. Sooner or later something comes up that shows who they really are. It took only three days for Joshua to discover that the Gibeonites had deceived him. It may take three days, three weeks, three months or three years for you to discover the truth about people who are pretending to love you.

And when the inhabitants of Gibeon heard what Joshua had done unto Jericho and to Ai,

They did work wilily, and went and made as if they had been ambassadors, and took old sacks upon their asses, and wine bottles, old, and rent, and bound up;

And old shoes and clouted upon their feet, and old garments upon them; and all the bread of their provision was dry and mouldy.

And they went to Joshua unto the camp at Gilgal, and said unto him, and to the men of Israel, We be come from a far country: now therefore make ye a league with us. . . .

And Joshua made peace with them, and made a league with them, to let them live: and the princes of the congregation sware unto them.

And it came to pass at the end of three days after they had made a league with them, that they heard that they were their neighbours, and that they dwelt among them.

Joshua 9:3-6, 15-16

4. Pretenders give themselves away many times and you must believe the signs you see.

Delilah revealed who she was on many occasions before she destroyed him. Samson found out that she was pretending but he did not take it seriously.

And Delilah said to Samson, Tell me, I pray thee, wherein thy great strength lieth, and wherewith thou mightest be bound to afflict thee.

And Samson said unto her, If they bind me with seven green withs that were never dried, then shall I be weak, and be as another man.

Then the lords of the Philistines brought up to her seven green withs which had not been dried, and she bound him with them.

Now there were men lying in wait, abiding with her in the chamber. And she said unto him, The Philistines be upon thee, Samson. And he brake the withs, as a thread of tow

16

is broken when it toucheth the fire. So his strength was not known.

And Delilah said unto Samson, Behold, thou hast mocked me, and told me lies: now tell me, I pray thee, wherewith thou mightest be bound.

Judges 16:6-10

5. A pretender is someone you cannot be at ease with.

And SHE MADE HIM SLEEP UPON HER KNEES; and she called for a man, and she caused him to shave off the seven locks of his head; and she began to afflict him, and his strength went from him.

Judges 16:18-19

You must not trust people whom you suspect to be pretenders. You must not relax in their presence. You cannot afford to be at ease or to trust your life to them. Samson slept on her knees and that was the last enjoyable sleep he had on this earth.

One day, a man of God was signing some of his books in the presence of some other staff. He was so exhausted because he had been ministering all day. When he finished he sat back, relaxed and started chatting with those around him. Some months later, one of the staff members who was there during the book signing re-described what had happened. He said the man of God was arrogant and laughed about how much money he earned every time he signed a book.

Obviously the man of God should not chat nor relax in the presence of such a person. Such people will misunderstand everything and re-present everything. It is important to know who to be at ease with.

6. Men are good at pretending towards women and women are good at pretending towards men.

Because of the differences between males and females, you must always be conscious of the possibility that someone of the opposite sex is pretending. Men are often taken in by women and women are often taken in by men.

Women Impress the Men

A good leader must be conscious of this when he is dealing with the opposite sex. We the men are quickly impressed and ravished with the beauty and soft voices of the ladies. We can hardly believe that any bad thing could come out of this pretty, harmless and fragile-looking girl. But within that harmless looking sleeping snake, lies the venomous power that can kill seventeen grown men.

Similarly, men impress women far more easily than they impress each other.

The words of Shakespeare in his book *Julius Caesar* are worth noting here. *"It is the bright day that brings forth the adder…"*

This means that a sunny bright day is attractive and welcoming to all who want to go out to enjoy nature. But it is the same bright day that attracts venomous deadly snakes out of their holes.

7. High expectations cause ministers of the gospel to pretend.

Woe unto you, scribes and Pharisees, hypocrites! for ye are like unto whited sepulchres, which indeed appear beautiful outward, but are within full of dead men's bones, and of all uncleanness.

Even so ye also outwardly appear righteous unto men, but within ye are full of hypocrisy and iniquity."

Matthew 23:27-28

The Pharisees are the best examples of ministers who pretend. On the outside they look white and beautiful, but on the inside everything is different. It is important to be the same on the outside as you are on the inside.

Ministers of the gospel often pretend about their marriages. Ministers also pretend about their spirituality because people want to feel that they are dealing with a super spiritual person. Ministers also pretend about miracles and about the power that they have. A minister of the gospel can grow and develop into a classic pretender.

8.   Children are good pretenders.

They put up a front to the parents and give the impression they are what they are not. Many parents have no idea who their children are and what they do. Sadly, many parents have lived to discover that their children were murderers or prostitutes. Even while at home many children pretend to be good whilst they are the worst of children.

> **Then Isaac said to Jacob, "Please come close, that I may feel you, my son, whether you are really my son Esau or not."**
>
> **So Jacob came close to Isaac his father, and he felt him and said, "The voice is the voice of Jacob, but the hands are the hands of Esau."**
>
> **And he did not recognize him, because his hands were hairy like his brother Esau's hands; so he blessed him.**
>
> **And he said, "Are you really my son Esau?" And he said, "I am."**
>
> **Genesis 27:21-24 (NASB)**

9.   A pretender is someone who can feign forgiveness.

Watch out for someone who you would expect to be angry and unforgiving because he has been wronged. Watch out for people who have been offended but seem to have completely ignored their offence and seem to be even more pleasing and gracious than before the offence occurred. You must always be sure that this person has genuinely forgiven you.

Jacob's sons pretended that they had forgiven the men who raped their sister. They turned around and amazingly offered their sister in marriage to the rapists. The rapists presumptuously assumed that they were accepted and loved by the brothers of the girl they had raped.

The Sons of Jacob Feign Forgiveness

But Jacob's sons answered Shechem and his father Hamor, WITH DECEIT, and spoke to them, because he had defiled Dinah their sister.

And they said to them, "We cannot do this thing, to give our sister to one who is uncircumcised, for that would be a disgrace to us.

"Only on this *condition* will we consent to you: if you will become like us, in that every male of you be circumcised, then we will give our daughters to you, and we will take your daughters for ourselves, and we will live with you and become one people.

"But if you will not listen to us to be circumcised, then we will take our daughter and go."

Now their words seemed reasonable to Hamor and Shechem, Hamor's son.

And the young man did not delay to do the thing, because he was delighted with Jacob's daughter. Now he was more respected than all the household of his father.

So Hamor and his son Shechem came to the gate of their city, and spoke to the men of their city, saying,

"These men are friendly with us; therefore let them live in the land and trade in it, for behold, the land is large enough for them. Let us take their daughters in marriage, and give our daughters to them.

"Only on this *condition* will the men consent to us to live with us, to become one people: that every male among us be circumcised as they are circumcised.

"Will not their livestock and their property and all their animals be ours? Only let us consent to them, and they will live with us."

And all who went out of the gate of his city listened to Hamor and to his son Shechem, and every male was circumcised, all who went out of the gate of his city.

Now it came about on the third day, when they were in pain, that two of Jacob's sons, Simeon and Levi, Dinah's brothers, each took his sword and came upon the city unawares, and killed every male.

And they killed Hamor and his son Shechem with the edge of the sword, and took Dinah from Shechem's house, and went forth."

Genesis 34:13-26 (NASB)

10. Pretenders have complete changes in attitude that seem unusual.

Jacob's sons seemed to have a sudden change in attitude towards the people who had raped their sister. Watch out for these sudden and unexplained changes in people's attitude. There may be a reason for sudden cheerfulness and exuberance! Always ask yourself why people are eager to do things for you. Could there be some other reason that makes them so excited and zealous?

11. Needy people are good candidates for pretence.

People who are looking for promotion and favours tend to bend over backwards to get what they want. They often find themselves pretending to their bosses and to any important person who can give them the favours they need. Watch poor and needy people carefully. Many people will pay any price to get ahead in life. Many people are prepared to "lick the bottoms" of the boss so that they will be liked. Tamar pretended to be a prostitute so that she could get the attention of her father-in-law.

Tamar Pretends to Be a Widow

And it was told Tamar, saying, Behold thy father in law goeth up to Timnath to shear his sheep.

And she put her widow's garments off from her, and covered her with a vail, and wrapped herself, and sat in an open place, which is by the way to Timnath; for she saw that Shelah was grown, and she was not given unto him to wife.

When Judah saw her, he thought her to be an harlot; because she had covered her face.

And he turned unto her by the way, and said, Go to, I pray thee, let me come in unto thee; (for he knew not that she was his daughter in law.) And she said, What wilt thou give me, that thou mayest come in unto me?

And he said, I will send thee a kid from the flock. And she said, Wilt thou give me a pledge, till thou send it?

And he said, What pledge shall I give thee? And she said, Thy signet, and thy bracelets, and thy staff that is in thine hand. And he gave it her, and came in unto her, and she conceived by him.

And she arose, and went away, and laid by her vail from her, and put on the garments of her widowhood."

Genesis 38:13-19

12. Someone who has served you for a short time has the potential to be a pretender.

Every leader must surround himself with loyal people. Some of these people will become friends, assistant pastors, counsellors or workers. The words of the people around you will make a lot of difference. The Scripture shows us that purposes are established through good counsel. What God has decided to do with your life will only be accomplished with good inputs and wise counsel from the people around you.

Ministers who depend solely on supernatural things usually do not do well. This is because we operate both in natural and spiritual dimensions. Large aspects of what we will do in the ministry will involve the natural and the physical.

Good inputs in all fields from loyal people make the difference to your life and ministry. Legal advice, medical advice and technical advice in various fields are crucial to success in ministry. We need the anointing but we also need the inputs of loyal people.

We need both the power and the wisdom of God. I dare say much of the failure in ministry comes about through the absence of good advice.

Select from among you seven men of good reputation, full of the Spirit and of wisdom, whom we may put in charge of this task" (Acts 6:3). Let's get back to our discussion on advisors who make a difference for the ministry.

The counsel of Hushai the Archite is better than the counsel of Ahithophel.

2 Samuel 17:14, NASB

Hushai was the quintessential impostor who pretended to give good advice to the king of the day. Because Absalom did not understand what I am teaching in this chapter, he was completely taken in by the pretence of Hushai. When you do not see through disloyal pretenders it can lead to your downfall. Lots of people are pretending all the time and a good leader must see through pretence.

Many times you cannot tell whether the advice of one person is better than the other. Most ministers do not have the ability to understand and relate with different subjects and fields of learning. Some ministers have no idea about legal things and so have to depend on the input of others.

Think of the legal, architectural, accounting, engineering, financial, human resource, computer and even medical aspects of life which affect your life. How can you be successful if you did not have the right advice in any of these fields?

I always remember the story of the prophet Branham who was the most humble and simple of the healing evangelists, having and owning very little. However, he was the one who was taken to court for tax issues and owed the state until he died.

23

Obviously, the people who surrounded him and advised him in these areas did not protect and help him.

Then Absalom and all the men of Israel said, "THE COUNSEL OF HUSHAI THE ARCHITE IS BETTER THAN THE COUNSEL OF AHITHOPHEL." For the LORD had ordained to thwart the good counsel of Ahithophel, so that the LORD might bring calamity on Absalom.

2 Samuel 17:14, NASB

Absalom set out to become the king of Israel. He almost succeeded in this quest but failed because he followed wrong advice. In the Scripture above, Absalom declared that the advice of Hushai was better than the advice of Ahithophel. But was it really better? Absalom's plan had taken years to develop. His plan worked beautifully until he followed a pretender's advice.

Absalom had two options: he had to choose between the advice of Ahithophel the Gillonite and the advice of Hushai the Archite. He made the crucial mistake of choosing Hushai as his advisor even though Ahithophel's advice was the best advice he could have had.

"And the counsel of Ahithophel, which he counseled in those days, was as if a man had inquired at the oracle of God: so was all the counsel of Ahithophel both with David and with Absalom" (2 Samuel 16:23).

Indeed, the advice of Ahithophel to Absalom was like the superior wisdom of God. But why was Absalom confused? Why did he make the mistake of choosing the advice of Hushai the Archite instead of taking the advice of Ahithophel the Gilonite?

The truth about counsel is that there are many ways to do the same thing. Each method and each suggestion has pros and cons. It is not always easy to know which way is better. Sometimes, it does seem impossible to distinguish between good and bad advice.

Ahithophel's Plan

Ahithophel presented Absalom with a good plan that promised to wipe out his father, David, forever.

"Furthermore, Ahithophel said to Absalom, 'Please let me choose twelve thousand men that I may arise and pursue David tonight.

I will come upon him while he is weary and exhausted and terrify him, so that all the people who are with him will flee. Then I will strike down the king alone, and I will bring back all the people to you. The return of everyone depends on the man you seek; then all the people will be at peace.' So the plan pleased Absalom and all the elders of Israel" (2 Samuel 17:1-4 NASB).

Hushai's Plan

Hushai also presented Absalom with an equally good plan, which had great promise of victory. "So Hushai said to Absalom, "This time the advice that Ahithophel has given is not good."

Moreover, Hushai said, "You know your father and his men, that they are mighty men and they are fierce, like a bear robbed of her cubs in the field. And your father is an expert in warfare, and will not spend the night with the people.

Behold, he has now hidden himself in one of the caves or in another place; and it will be when he falls on them at the first attack, that whoever hears it will say, 'There has been a slaughter among the people who follow Absalom.'

And even the one who is valiant, whose heart is like the heart of a lion, will completely lose heart; for all Israel knows that your father is a mighty man and those who are with him are valiant men.

But I counsel that all Israel be surely gathered to you, from Dan even to Beersheba, as the sand that is by the sea in abundance, and that you personally go into battle.

So we shall come to him in one of the places where he can be found, and we will fall on him as the dew falls on the ground; and of him and of all the men who are with him, not even one will be left.

If he withdraws into a city, then all Israel shall bring ropes to that city, and we will drag it into the valley until not even a small stone is found there" (2 Samuel 17:7-13 NASB).

Which Plan Was Better?

As you can see both plans sound good and few people would have been able to distinguish the good from the bad. However, one principle could have saved Absalom; the principle of preferring a loyal person's input to the advice of someone of unproven loyalties. Absalom should have chosen to listen to the advice of someone he had known for a long time.

Ahithophel was a long-standing supporter of the conspiracy to overthrow King David. Absalom actually sent for Ahithophel when it was time to overthrow King David. He was the person Absalom should have listened to.

Absalom would have been safer with anything that Ahithophel proposed because he had already proved that he was on his side. "And Absalom sent for Ahithophel the Gilonite, David's counselor, from his city Giloh, while he offered sacrifices. And the conspiracy was strong, for the people increased continually with Absalom" (2 Samuel 15:12).

The advice of Hushai was lengthier and more impressive. It involved more options and counter proposals in case anything went wrong. Ahithophel's advice was brief and not as impressive as Hushai's. Unfortunately, many people listen to new and flashy counsellors rather than depending on old faithful people whose loyalties have been proven over the years.

This is a fatal mistake and it is on this very point that many ministries and even businesses begin a downward spiral. I prefer to listen to old faithful people who have demonstrated that they love me and believe in me.

13. A pretender hesitates to implement his own ideas.

Follow the advice of someone who is prepared to implement what he is suggesting. Absalom failed to recognize this. If he had known this, he would have chosen to listen to Ahithophel rather than to Hushai.

There are people who give advice but will not help to carry it out. In fact, they have no idea about how to carry out their own instructions.

Ahithophel made a suggestion and offered to carry it out himself. That was significant. "Moreover Ahithophel said unto Absalom, **LET ME** now choose out twelve thousand men, and **I WILL ARISE** and pursue after David this night: And **I WILL COME** upon him while he is weary and weak handed, and will make him afraid: and all the people that are with him shall flee; and **I WILL SMITE** the king only: And **I WILL BRING** back all the people unto thee: the man whom thou seekest is as if all returned: so all the people shall be in peace. And the saying pleased Absalom well, and all the elders of Israel" (2 Samuel 17:1-4).

But notice the advice that Hushai the Archite gave. First of all, he never offered to help Absalom carry out the plan. He rather advised Absalom to endanger himself by going out into battle himself.

Unfortunately, Absalom could not see that he was being sent to his own death. "But I counsel that all Israel be surely gathered to you, from Dan even to Beersheba, as the sand that is by the sea in abundance, and that **YOU PERSONALLY GO INTO BATTLE**" (2 Samuel 17:11 NASB).

Anytime I receive a suggestion, I often ask the person suggesting it to carry it out himself. That is how to determine if the advice is usable or not.

Unfortunately, many people are not practical and cannot build anything. They may have certificates from school, but they cannot translate what they have learnt in school into reality.

Many churches are run by priests with theological certificates. However, these certificates do not necessarily help the church to grow. Likewise, many nations are run by theoreticians with university degrees. Unfortunately, a degree from school means very little when it comes to real nation building.

You must learn to distinguish between people who talk a lot with high-sounding ideas and people who bring practical solutions. Surround yourself with people who solve problems and make things happen practically.

14. A pretender can be known by the fear and panic he generates.

Hushai was a wise man and he knew he had to frighten Absalom away from the path of success. Hushai's advice incited much fear. Hushai spoke of several things that frightened Absalom and his followers.

He reminded Absalom and the other rebellious elders that David was a very experienced soldier - a winner of many battles. He asked Absalom to remember the kind of person his father was. He described David as a bear. And not an ordinary bear, but a female bear robbed of her cubs! That is not an animal anyone would like to meet!

> **Moreover, Hushai said, "You know your father and his men, that they are mighty men and they are fierce, like a bear robbed of her cubs in the field. And your father is an expert in warfare... "**
>
> **2 Samuel 17:8, NASB**

He also reminded them of the kind of mighty men that were with David. A list of these mighty men in 2 Samuel 23 would send chills down the spine of any brave warrior. Hushai told Absalom to watch out for terrible fighters like Joab the commander and Abishai, his brother, who killed three hundred men in one go.

Hushai reminded Absalom of Adino the Eznite, who killed eight hundred people at one time. Then he told him not to forget about Benaiah the son of Jehoiada, who killed a lion in the middle of a pit on a snowy day. What about Abishai, who killed Goliath's brother?

After listening to an unsettling account of these mighty men, Absalom was frightened. This same thing happened to the children of Israel when they first attempted to enter the Promised Land. They heard of the giants and were frightened away from the Promised Land. They backed off from their God-given heritage because of the frightening details they heard. You will never do well as long as you listen to advice that inspires fear.

Jesus said to Jairus, "Fear not, only believe." Jesus always comes with "Fear not." It is the devil who inspires fear. Watch out for prophets who are always telling you bad things about the future and frightening you. God is telling you to beware of things that create fear in your heart. Fear not, only believe!

Listen to Can-Do Advice

Ahithophel's advice was "can-do" advice! It was positive! It was practical! It was possibility thinking. It was advice that could be followed immediately. Most things that can be done can be done now!

Let's Marry Right Now!

Years ago, when I met my wife, I told her that I wanted to marry her *immediately*. I really desired to marry her as soon as practical. I felt that I had made up my mind and there was no more reason to delay. "Let's get on with it and get married!"

I thought she would be unsettled by my insistence on us marrying soon. But she wasn't. One day, she told me something that surprised me. She said, "My father says that if a man will really marry you, he will want to marry you right now."

Through experience, her father had realized that good young suitors often had the desire to marry at once.

Now, in my own experience, I have noticed that men who say, "I will marry you in the next four years", "I will marry you when I come back from my five-year post-graduate program", do not usually get married as promised.

Always remember: Advice that can be implemented immediately is usually good advice!

Ahithophel's Advice to Absalom Generates Strength

Ahithophel's advice was based on his understanding of human behaviour. He wanted Absalom to do things that would encourage the troops. He knew that the psychological strength of the people on the mission would make or break them.

Ahithophel wanted Absalom to sleep with his father's wives so that his rebellious troops would sense the determination of their leader and be strengthened by it.

"Then Absalom said to Ahithophel, "Give your advice. What shall we do?" Ahithophel said to Absalom, "Go in to your father's concubines, whom he has left to keep the house; then all Israel will hear that you have made yourself odious to your father. THE HANDS OF ALL WHO ARE WITH YOU WILL ALSO BE STRENGTHENED So they pitched a tent for Absalom on the roof, and Absalom went in to his father's concubines in the sight of all Israel" (2 Samuel 16: 20-22 NASB).

When Ahithophel suggested that Absalom sleep with his father's wives, it was not because he wanted Absalom to taste King David's exclusive and exquisite sexual delights. This was certainly not the time for relaxation or sexual pleasure. It was time for boosting the morale of the troops.

It was time to win the confidence of the troops and to succeed in their mission. It was time to let the troops know that they were following a strong, determined and fearless leader!

The next bit of Ahithophel's advice was also based on the concept of strengthening and stabilizing his followers.

... and I will bring back all the people to you. The return of everyone depends on the man you seek; THEN ALL THE PEOPLE WILL BE AT PEACE.
2 Samuel 17:3, NASB

You cannot build a church unless the people following you have peace and a sense of well-being. You must do things that make them feel strengthened in their mission. If the people who follow you have no sense of security, they will soon give up.

Years ago, I was the leader of a small group of students, which was developing into a church. When it became apparent that I did not intend to leave the country or the church, the people who followed me were strengthened and became more committed. The church grew and became established. We grew out of our little classroom and became a mega church.

Building a team of full-time workers and missionaries will require much of Ahithophel's kind of wisdom. Without peace and a sense of well-being, people will constantly abandon ship.

There is something that I call *"a feel well item"*. I have learned over the years that the administration of these *"feel well items"* dramatically boosts the morale of the troops. Every leader should learn to do things that bring encouragement, peace and well-being to his followers. The "feel well" environment is not created by splashing money around. The Holy Spirit will guide you into what is a feel well item.

People have remarked about the number of medical doctors, engineers, lawyers, gold miners and highly qualified people who have abandoned their jobs to follow me into ministry. These people work for me willingly for a small fraction of what they would have earned in the world. I have watched as highly paid professionals in the USA and Europe abandoned what they were doing, came to Africa and worked for virtually nothing.

I do not have much money to offer them but they seem to be eager and blessed to work in the ministry. This is not my doing because I did not plan or engineer it. Looking back however, I realize how God's grace has brought about the Ahithophel kind of wisdom to make His will possible.

15. A pretender can be identified by his impractical suggestions.

Ahithophel's plan hinged on targeting one person, King David. This is an eternal principle that guarantees success in almost any endeavour. Ahithophel tried to explain that the outcome of the entire operation depended on taking on one person.

Pastors will accomplish more if they target the right people. Ministering to large numbers and targeting multitudes is great. However, if you want real growth you will have to focus on a few individuals who can fulfil the vision.

"… and I will bring back all the people to you. The return of everyone DEPENDS ON THE MAN YOU SEEK; then all the people will be at peace." (2 Samuel 17:3 NASB)

Many people feel that strength comes from targeting large numbers. Ahithophel targeted only one man, King David. Hushai suggested that they eliminate David and all the men that were with him. Ahithophel targeted one person and Hushai targeted the multitude of mighty men.

This grandiose idea sounded more promising as it would get rid of all the mighty men who were loyal to David. "So we shall come to him in one of the places where he can be found, and we will fall on him as the dew falls on the ground; and OF HIM AND OF ALL THE MEN WHO ARE WITH HIM, NOT EVEN ONE WILL BE LEFT" (2 Samuel 17:12 NASB). How impressive! Not even one of David's mighty men would have been left if this plan had been executed.

When King David fought back at Absalom, this principle was taken into account and David was not allowed to go into the battle. They told him, "If they even kill half of us, it will not matter, but if you die, that will be the end of all of us." "And the king said to the people, "I myself will surely go out with you also." But the people said, "You should not go out; for if we indeed flee, they will not care about us; even if half of us die, they will not care about us. But you are worth ten thousand of us; therefore now it is better that you be ready to help us from the city"(2 Samuel 18:2-3 NASB).

Now, this was a war between David's army and Absalom's army. Absalom followed the bad advice of Hushai to go out himself whilst David followed good advice and stayed at home. Simply put, this became a war between the wise and the foolish.

Just as Ahithophel predicted, the war ended when one man was killed. And Absalom was the one man whose death ended the war! Ahithophel knew that everything hinged on what happened to one person. "And ten young men who carried Joab's armor gathered around and struck Absalom and killed him. Then Joab blew the trumpet, and the people returned from pursuing Israel, for Joab restrained the people" (2 Samuel 18:15-16 NASB). As soon as Absalom was dead, the conflict was over.

Perhaps, it is this principle that most of us fail to see. If we were able to reach the one person that God has called us to, we would accomplish much more. Because we love the pomp and fame that come with doing programmes with groups, we do not spend time on the individuals who can make all the difference.

Every leader should do what it takes to build his ministry. Do what you have to do! Spend time with the few you need to spend time with. Many people's lives depend on your ability to choose a few key people and invest in them. Make some people special because there will always be special people. They are special to your life and to your survival!

The devil seems to know the wisdom of Ahithophel better than most Christians. That is why he attacks believers one at a time. He is not so worried about the church you belong to. He will take you up when you are alone. "Be sober, be vigilant; because your adversary the devil, as a roaring lion, walketh about, seeking whom he may devour" (1 Peter 5:8).

Lions hunt down their prey one at a time. You will never find a lion targeting seventeen antelopes at the same time.

Satan Targets Individuals One at a Time

Satan is seeking to destroy key leaders on whom much depends. You may look weak when you don't do certain things. A leader may look wasteful when certain amounts of money are spent on him.

I am sure that some would have accused Absalom of being a coward for not going into battle himself. Nevertheless, he was a fool to go and it cost him his life when he went.

Sometimes, the difficulties you go through as a person are because of the position of leadership you are in. If you were not occupying that all-important chair, you would not experience one tenth of your current problems.

There are financial problems that will beset you because you are in that special position. The media will harass you because of your position in the ministry.

There are serious marital problems that may plague you just because of your role in the ministry. I have watched pastors who have had beautiful marriages begin to have serious problems when they moved higher in the ministry.

Higher levels usually attract higher devils. Kings and "immortal" leaders have died because they were the sole target of almost every attack.

Ahab, the famous husband of Jezebel, fought a battle in which he was the sole target. That is the battle that ended his life!

And the king of Israel said unto Jehoshaphat, I will disguise myself, and enter into the battle; but put thou on thy robes. And the king of Israel disguised himself, and went into the battle.

But the king of Syria commanded his thirty and two captains that had rule over his chariots, saying, FIGHT NEITHER WITH SMALL NOR GREAT, SAVE ONLY WITH THE KING of Israel.

And it came to pass, when the captains of the chariots saw Jehoshaphat, that they said, Surely it is the king of Israel. And they turned aside to fight against him: and Jehoshaphat cried out.

And it came to pass, when the captains of the chariots perceived that it was not the king of Israel, that they turned back from pursuing him.

And a certain man drew a bow at a venture, and smote the king of Israel between the joints of   the harness:

1 Kings 22:30-34

Ahab was the sole target of that war. The king or leader is the light of the group he leads.

David was called the light of Israel and that was why he was treated specially. "But Abishai the son of Zeruiah succoured him, and smote the Philistine, and killed him. Then the men of David sware unto him, saying, Thou shalt go no more out with us to battle, that thou quench not the light of Israel" (2 Samuel 21:17).

Never forget that the leader is the light of the group he leads. If the light is quenched, darkness will descend on everyone that follows him.

16. A pretender pretends that you need large numbers of people to lead when you need one person to be successful.

There are people who want things to be done through groups and committees. "You cannot trust one person with such power," they say. "It is too dangerous for one person to have such authority." Indeed, these high-sounding concepts of safety, maturity and the plurality of leadership look like real wisdom. But the Word of God teaches how many things can be accomplished through one key person. Achieving goals through groups, committees and large numbers of people is an attractive option to some people.

But I have experienced much success by working with one key person on every project. God's Word shows us that he searches for one person and works through one person. "And I sought for A MAN among them, that should make up the hedge, and stand in the gap before me for the land, that I should not destroy it: but I found none" (Ezekiel 22:30).

Absalom wanted to know what both Ahithophel and Hushai thought on the matter. Both advisors spoke and once again, Absalom had two options to choose from.

Hushai, who was intentionally giving bad advice told Absalom to work through thousands of people. "But I COUNSEL THAT ALL ISRAEL BE SURELY GATHERED TO YOU, from Dan even to Beersheba, as the sand that is by the sea in abundance, and that you personally go into battle" (2 Samuel 17:11, NASB).

Ahithophel however offered to seek out the king and eliminate him personally. "Ahithophel said to Absalom, Please let me choose 12,000 men that I MAY arise and pursue David tonight. I WILL come upon him while he is weary and exhausted and terrify him, so that all the people who are with him will flee. Then I WILL strike down the king alone" (2 Samuel 17:1-2 NASB).

Can you see why Absalom would prefer Hushai's advice? Hushai's plan was to fight a war with thousands and thousands of people who numbered like the sand of the sea. Ahithophel's plan involved only twelve thousand men and him personally assassinating King David.

Unfortunately, Absalom opted to accomplish his purpose through large numbers of people. I can see how working with larger groups is more attractive. Preaching to big congregations gives you the feeling that you are doing more.

Somehow, Jesus seemed to think otherwise; that is why he spent more time with his disciples than with the large crowds. He knew that everything depended on one person.

That is why He said, "It is written, I will smite the shepherd, and the sheep of the flock shall be scattered abroad" (Matthew 26:31).

Most of the teachings that we read from the book of John were given to the small group of disciples. From the fifth chapter of John, Jesus' focused his ministry on the twelve disciples and not on the multitudes.

God has blessed me with individuals through whom I work. I am engaged in different unrelated areas of ministry. However, I tackle each area through the help of just one person. Whatever I build, I do through one person.

I do not attempt to build a church unless I have one man - the pastor. If I want to have a mission to a foreign nation, all I need is one person - the missionary. I do not depend on getting the commitment and approval of several people.

I need only one person to establish a new department. I do not depend on teams or groups. This has worked best for me. That is the Ahithophel kind of wisdom which is also the oracle of God for you!

Years ago, I established a music group called "The BeeDees". I wanted to build a wonderful team of musicians who would sing and play together. After a while, everyone went in different directions and the group disintegrated. I was very disappointed to say the least.

However, I realized that I could never accomplish my vision for music through a group. Now, I work with individuals and that is much easier.

17. A pretender can be identified by his love for procrastination and delays.

A crucial aspect of Ahithophel's plan was to attack David without delay.

King David was a strong fighter but he was not invincible neither was he immortal. Naturally, given the right conditions, King David could be defeated. Ahithophel knew exactly when and how David could be defeated and he said so. "Ahithophel said to Absalom, Please let me choose 12,000 men that I may arise and pursue David TONIGHT" (2 Samuel 17:1 NASB).

The key word here is *"tonight"*. It was important that Absalom pursue David at that particular time. Ahithophel knew that conditions were favourable only for that night.

What conditions made that night favourable for Absalom?

David was weary and exhausted and Ahithophel wanted the attack to come on during David's lowest moment "I will come upon him WHILE HE IS WEARY AND EXHAUSTED and terrify him, so that all the people who are with him will flee. Then I will strike down the king alone" (2 Samuel 17:2).

Hushai also knew that David was weary and exhausted and he wanted to buy some time for David. That is why he asked him to wait until thousands and thousands of troops could gather. Can you imagine how long it took to assemble all these troops?

The Right Timing

Dear friend, there is a time to every purpose. If you miss the timing, you are not likely to succeed. Whilst you are on this earth, everything you do will depend on doing it at the right time.

God may have chosen you to have the largest church in your country. But perhaps, the right time to begin this great ministry is when you are twenty-five years old. If you delay and begin when you are forty-five years old, the vision will be greatly affected.

Wrong timing makes things look as though it is not God's will. Many times it is the will of God but the wrong time.

Ahithophel advised Absalom to attack when David was tired. He knew that Absalom's only chance was when his father was physically exhausted.

Why was Ahithophel's advice more genuine than Hushai's? Because Ahithophel's advice was to accomplish the vision "now". "Now" is the time for most great visions!

18. A pretender is known by his lack of depth of thought, strength and timing.

Real strength comes from the Lord. Pretenders do not have real deep commitment. This is seen by their failure to acquire real strength for the work they have to do. A minister of the gospel who is not genuine does not wait on the Lord to acquire real strength.

There are battles that every strong leader will lose just because he is exhausted. That is why God wants us to have retreats and camps to strengthen ourselves. Your ministry will be transformed when you have camps.

Hushai knew that David would have a camp and become strong enough to fight against Absalom. He misled Absalom into allowing David the privilege of having a camp to strengthen himself. David had a camp at a place called Mahanaim and the camp director was Barzillai, the Gileadite.

"And Israel and Absalom camped in the land of Gilead. Now when David had come to Mahanaim, Shobi the son of Nahash from Rabbah of the sons of Ammon, Machir the son of Ammiel from Lo-debar, and Barzillai the Gileadite from Rogelim, brought beds, basins, pottery, wheat, barley, flour, parched grain, beans, lentils, parched seeds, honey, curds, sheep, and cheese of the herd, for David and for the people who were with him, to eat; for they said, 'The people are hungry and weary and thirsty in the wilderness'" (2 Samuel 17:26-29).

"Now Barzillai was very old, being eighty years old; and he had sustained the king while he stayed at Mahanaim, for he was a very great man" (2 Samuel 19:32). Later on, King David rewarded Barzillai the Gileadite for his help in refreshing them.

Through the advice of Hushai the pretender, Absalom gave David enough time to rest and to eat bread, beans, meat, honey etc. By the time Absalom got his act together, Barzillai, the Gileadite had brought him all the food, basins and beds that he needed.

Don't try fighting David after he has eaten bread, cheese, beans, parched grain and beef. It was a fatal mistake to take on David's mighty men after they had eaten. It was simply the wrong time to fight someone like David and his mighty men. Absalom should have fought them when they were tired and hungry. He missed the right time and lost everything.

Can you imagine the strength that Adino the Eznite, (a killer of eight hundred people) would have after eating a whole sheep? Can you imagine how strong Abishai, (the killer of Goliath's brother) would have felt after eating a whole goat?

It is important that you understand that success and failure depend greatly on timing. May the Holy Spirit guide you into knowing the time for His purposes. Absalom failed because he allowed his enemy to develop the strength that he needed. Which part of your ministry is failing because of poor timing?

Do not set yourself up for discouragement by embarking on things that you are not ready for.

Do not launch out into fields that are not ripened for harvest.

CHAPTER 3

Intimidation and Disloyalty

Intimidation is the art of DETERRING or controlling someone THROUGH FEAR.

1. **Intimidation is a powerful force that controls and deters God's servants by making them afraid of something real or imagined.**

Intimidation is a real invisible, not easily defined, opposition to your ministry. Many ministers do not continue what God has told them to do because they are intimidated by trends that make the truth seem irrelevant and outdated.

In the text below, we see how Nehemiah refused to be intimidated by people inspired by the devil. Do not allow your ministry to be deterred or controlled by threats of any sort.

The fifth time, Sanballat's servant came with an open letter in his hand, and this is what it said: "Geshem tells me that everywhere he goes he hears that you and the Jews are planning to rebel and that is why you are building the wall. According to his reports, you plan to be their king.

He also reports that you have appointed prophets to prophesy about you in Jerusalem, saying, 'Look! There is a king in Judah!' "You can be very sure that this report will get back to the king, so I suggest that you come and talk it over with me."

My reply was, "You know you are lying. There is no truth in any part of your story."

THEY WERE JUST TRYING TO INTIMIDATE US, imagining that they could break our resolve and stop the work. So I prayed for strength to continue the work. Later I went to visit Shemaiah son of Delaiah and grandson of Mehetabel, who was confined to his home. He said, "Let us meet together inside the Temple of God and bolt the doors shut. Your enemies are coming to kill you tonight." But I replied, "Should someone in my position run away from danger? Should someone in my position enter the Temple to save his life? No, I won't do it!" I realized that God had not spoken to him, but that he had uttered this prophecy against me because Tobiah and Sanballat had hired him. THEY WERE HOPING TO INTIMIDATE ME AND MAKE ME SIN by following his suggestion. Then they would be able to accuse and discredit me" (Nehemiah 6:5-13, NLT).

Some years ago, I was invited to preach in a certain church that had thousands of members. I had never been there before and did not know what to expect.

A friend of mine heard that I had been invited to this great church and warned me that I had better preach a good message because if I did not preach a good message I would not receive a good honorarium.

He told he how he had preached in that same church before but had been told by the pastor that his sermon was not good enough. The pastor told him that the congregation did not enjoy his messages and therefore he was given a much-reduced honorarium.

I was immediately intimidated by this report. I wondered if I would be able to preach a good enough sermon. I wondered to myself, "What is a good sermon? What should I preach about? Should I preach about love or success? Should I preach about money and how to prosper? I knew people liked such messages."

I was desperate and frightened by the thought of my sermon being assessed in such a way by the pastors and the congregation. I needed a message that would make me liked and popular so that I could receive a good offering!

Then the Holy Spirit said to me, "Preach what I tell you. Preach the message I have given you."

Immediately, I was set free from the need to impress anyone.

What the Holy Spirit told me was my guiding post and I prayed for boldness to declare the message that the Lord had given me. Not caring what anyone thought, I preached on what the Lord told me to.

In the end I was glad that I was not intimidated by the threat of my sermon being assessed so critically. I was set free from the need to preach about love, success or prosperity. I preached the gospel and the power of God was manifested.

2. **Intimidation is to deter someone from some action by threatening to reveal some in-formation you have about them. The spirit of intimidation says, "I know you. I know all about you."**

Someone who does not know much about you cannot intimidate you. Intimidation comes from people who misuse the access they have been given. It is people who are familiar with you who can intimidate you. *The spirit of familiarity and the spirit of intimidation work together.*

And there was in their synagogue a man with an unclean spirit; and he cried out, Saying, Let us alone; what have we to do with thee, thou Jesus of Nazareth? Art thou come to destroy us? I KNOW THEE WHO THOU ART, the Holy One of God.

And Jesus rebuked him, saying, Hold thy peace, and come out of him.

Mark 1:23-25

I Know You Don't Have Miracles

I remember a young man who despised me and left our church. He told everyone, "That guy doesn't have any miracles. There is no power in the church."

I felt embarrassed about it. I felt impotent and useless. The critics continued, "He is just an administrator. He is a 'white man' without power who uses administrative techniques to help the church." I felt so inadequate and powerless as a pastor. I said to myself, "I do not compare with real ministers of the gospel in the world."

A couple of years later, God blessed me and I began having miracle services. Every time there were miracles, I would remember this person and how he mocked at me for having no miracles in my ministry.

3. **Intimidation is demonic in its origin. It is evil spirits that threaten to use information to deter or control you. Both Jesus and Paul were openly attacked by evil spirits that wanted to intimidate them.**

And it came to pass, as we went to prayer, a certain damsel possessed with a spirit of divination met us, which brought her masters much gain by soothsaying:

The same followed Paul and us, and cried, saying, these men are the servants of the Most High God, which shew unto us the way of salvation.

And this did she many days. But Paul, being grieved, turned and said to the spirit, I command thee in the name of Jesus Christ to come out of her. And he came out the same hour.

Acts 16:16-18

One night, in a foreign country, I was alone lying on my bed when I saw a huge naked black man about eight or nine feet tall standing at the foot of my bed. I immediately knew that I was seeing in the spirit and looking straight at the devil. I was terrified.

Suddenly, Satan began to cackle and to laugh at me. Then I noticed something unusual. The huge black man had the face of someone I had known before.

This person, had belonged to my church before but had mocked at me and made fun of my attempts to do the work of God.

At the time I had been greatly discouraged and intimidated by the things he said. In that terrifying vision I realised that intimidation was demonic and satanic. Satan is the author of intimidation.

The spirit of intimidation is the spirit of the devil. He seeks to deter you from serving the Lord. He seeks to prevent you from moving forward and venturing into new territories.

4. Intimidation is to deter someone from some action by frightening them about exposure of their past sins.

And there were seven sons of *one* Sceva, a Jew, and chief of the priests, which did so.

And the evil spirit answered and said, Jesus I know, and Paul I know; but who are ye?

And the man in whom the evil spirit was leaped on them, and overcame them, and prevailed against them, so that they fled out of that house naked and wounded.

Acts 19:14-16

God knows our past and the devil also knows our failures. How does the devil know all about our shameful past? Most of the shameful things we have done were inspired and guided by him. He was there to supervise you and ensure that you fulfilled his vision for shameful and disgraceful deeds.

Is it any wonder that he has a dossier on all of us? Satan inspires people who know about our past sins to intimidate and frighten us.

You will notice in the New Testament that the favourite remark of the evil spirits that spoke out during the ministries of Jesus and Paul was, *"I know you."*

Evil spirits know things that human beings do not know because they can see things that human beings cannot see. Evil spirits know history better than any human being because they have been around for thousands of years and have seen mankind go through his cycles.

The evil spirits kept revealing the identity of Christ in a way that He did not like. Revealing your identity at the wrong time is very dangerous and can destroy you. That is why the Lord kept silencing the evil spirits who blurted out His identity.

Similarly, Paul was confronted with evil spirits who kept announcing his identity at the wrong place and time.

When the seven sons of Sceva attempted to cast out devils they were met with knowledgeable demons that refused to budge.

"Who are you?" they said. "We know who Paul is and we know who Jesus is. But you do not qualify to speak to us in that tone of voice."

And with that they gave them a sound thrashing and stripped them naked.

5. Intimidation is to deter someone from some action by frightening them with exposure of the *uncomely aspects* of their lives.

And those *members* of the body, which we think to be less honourable, upon these we bestow more abundant honour; and our uncomely *parts* have more abundant comeliness.

For our comely *parts* have no need: but God hath tempered

the body together, having given more abundant honour to that *part* which lacked:

1 Corinthians 12:23-24

Everyone has uncomely parts. There are things that are not sin but they are not beautiful nor are they suitable for public consumption. Uncomeliness is different from sin. The Bible speaks of members of the body which are comely and those that are uncomely, but equally important.

The spirit of intimidation loves to bring up aspects of our lives that are not nice to speak about. This is the spirit of embarrassment. Maybe you have a difficult marriage or a difficult child. Perhaps you have a personal weakness or an embarrassing sickness. The demons love to bring up these things to intimidate and deter you from freely ministering the Word of God.

Watch out for those who use their closeness to you and the knowledge they have gained about you against you! The demons knew that Jesus had a humble background, and that he came from a carpenter's family. The demons knew that there had been some controversy about the father of Mary's child. This is the kind of thing evil spirits love to play on!

Is not this the carpenter, the son of Mary, the brother of James, and Joses, and of Juda, and Simon? and are not his sisters here with us? And they were offended at him.

Mark 6: 3

A brother who had known me for years said to me, "I will write a book about you and drive you out of this city." Obviously, he knew that I was just a man who made mistakes like everyone else. He had known me for some years and he knew that I made mistakes like everyone else. As his hatred and rebellion boiled over, he threatened to fight me until I ran away with my tail between my legs. It was the spirit of intimidation speaking through that young man.

To have someone who has lived with you and been close to you for years threaten to speak about you in a certain way is intimidating, to say the least. None of us could stand the test of constant scrutiny on our lives. Very close screening of your every move and your every word will always reveal lapses in your character and personality.

When Michael Jackson died, psychologists were interviewed about his odd lifestyle and queer behaviour. I particularly remember the remarks of a psychologist who said: "It is not normal for someone to be under intense scrutiny for long periods."

She continued, "Such continuous scrutiny can break down any normal person and destroy him and this is what happened to Michael Jackson."

None of us could tolerate a twenty-four hour video camera filming every second of our day. We would have a nervous breakdown and beg for a few minutes of relief so that we could relax and not have to be so prim and proper all the time.

The Bible says, "If we say we have no sin we deceive ourselves and the truth is not is us." Who would like to have his mistakes, his slips, his errors, his missteps, and his deviations filmed and shown to the world? We thank God for the blood of Jesus.

Refuse to be intimidated by those who claim they know you! It is the same evil spirits that harassed Jesus, continually claiming they knew Him. "I know you, I know you," is the voice of demons intimidating, alarming and threatening you and your ministry.

6. Intimidation is to deter someone from some action by mocking, scoffing and despising him.

Sanballat described the wall Nehemiah was building as something that could be broken down by a little fox. He made fun of Nehemiah's wall saying it was worth nothing. But it was worth something. Don't listen to people who make fun of you and your ministry. It is the spirit of Sanballat intimidating you.

The wall that Nehemiah built became the world-famous Wall of Jerusalem. It will always be remembered and Nehemiah will always be remembered for his efforts. Sanballat's words were just a demonic attempt to stop him in his tracks.

Sanballat Looks Down on Nehemiah's Efforts

But it came to pass, that when Sanballat heard that we builded the wall, he was wroth, and took great indignation, and mocked the Jews.

And he spake before his brethren and the army of Samaria, and said, What do these feeble Jews? will they fortify themselves? will they sacrifice? will they make an end in a day? will they revive the stones out of the heaps of the rubbish which are burned?

Now Tobiah the Ammonite was by him, and he said, Even that which they build, if a fox go up, he shall even break down their stone wall.

Hear, O our God; for we are despised: and turn their reproach upon their own head, and give them for a prey in the land of captivity:

Nehemiah 4:1-4

How is the Students' Fellowship?

Years ago, when we started our church, there was a man of God who had a church in a nearby hall. He happened to see all our efforts to begin the church and he knew that our new church was called Korle-Bu Christian Centre.

One day, I met him in town and asked him, "How is your church doing?" He said, "Fine, it's doing well."

Then he asked, "How is your students' fellowship?" I wanted to protest and say, "It's not a students' fellowship. It is a church and you know we have started a church." But I had to swallow my words and answer his humbling question.

So I said, "The students' fellowship is fine."

I felt demeaned and intimidated. I had heard the devil's voice saying to me, "It is not a church. It will never be a church. It is a students' fellowship and it will always be just a fellowship."

But I refused to be intimidated and continued to press on to build the little church until it became a mega church.

Do not allow anyone to demean your efforts to build a church!

It is going to work in the end!

Though your beginning is small your latter end will be greatly increased!

You Have Twelve Cells

The devil does not cease to intimidate (deter) you when you attempt to make progress in the Lord. The time came when the Lord led me to begin branches of our church.

One day, a visiting pastor asked about the progress of our ministry. We told him we were doing well and that we had twelve extra churches. Then he asked how many people there were in each church. We explained that some of them had ten members and others had twenty and some had fifty.

He then laughed and said, "You don't have twelve churches. You have twelve cell groups. Those are not churches, they are cells!"

I felt so embarrassed when this man of God made fun of our churches. But as we persisted with these little branches they grew into mighty trees with hundreds and thousands of members. Do not be intimidated by the mocking statements of fellow ministers of the gospel. Continue doing what God has called you to do. It will work in the end.

7. Intimidation will keep you from pressing into new areas of ministry.

Intimidation is an evil spirit sent to alarm you, terrify you and push you around. Satan wants to confine you to the limits he has defined for you. But you must break out.

Sanballat and Tobiah wanted Nehemiah to go back to Persia. They did not want him to engage in new ideas so they kept intimidating him. Do not forget the definition of intimidation: *Intimidation is the art of deterring someone through fear.* Satan wants to deter you from new ideas, new visions and new territories. That is why he is alarming you, frightening you and warding you off.

> ...And Tobiah sent many threatening letters to intimidate me.
>
> Nehemiah 6:19 (NLT)

> They were just trying to intimidate us, imagining that they could break our resolve and stop the work. So I prayed for strength to continue the work.
>
> Nehemiah 6:9 (NLT)

Intimidation Whilst Building a New Church

Beginning a church was no small experience for me. I was intimidated at almost every juncture. Preaching sermons, conducting weddings, baptising people were all intimidating experiences that I had to overcome.

I always remember the first wedding I officiated. The parents of the groom were born-again Christians and they asked who was officiating the wedding. When they found out that it was yours truly, they just asked one question, "Is he powerful?"

When I heard that they were asking if I was a powerful minister, I was intimidated and I felt like running away. I did not want to officiate the wedding any more.

The spirit of the scoffer tries to stop you in your tracks. It comes to prevent you from going ahead with the vision that God has for you.

Through a combination of ridicule and mockery there will be no more spirit left in you to carry on in the ministry. That is why the Scripture says blessed is the man who does not sit in the seat of scoffers.

Moving into Baptisms

Satan keeps you away from boldly engaging in new things through the fear of ridicule and embarrassment. I remember the first time I baptized somebody. I fumbled with the first person to be baptized and before I realized, the person assisting me was laughing his head off!

I felt so embarrassed and have never forgotten that laugh! But I carried on baptizing and it got better.

Satan knows that feeling and he capitalizes on it anytime there is something new and bold to do. Ridicule is a barrier you must overcome.

The devil is a bully and he knows what will frighten you. Anytime you attempt to move into a new area of ministry, he reminds you of your inexperience and lack of power.

Do not allow anyone to intimidate you as you walk on new roads and into new territories.

8. It is a sin to intimidate the servants of the Lord.

It is a sin to intimidate someone by threatening or blackmailing them with information that you have about them. It is a sin in the eyes of God. The Lord knows the secrets and the secret sins of His servants. David, the sweet psalmist, would pray about his secret sins. "Thou hast set our iniquities before thee, our secret sins in the light of thy countenance" (Psalms 90:8).

Our sins are with the Lord and He knows what He is going to do with us. He is the judge and we stand or fall before Him. It is wickedness to take advantage of someone because you saw him in his weakness. It is this evil which both medicine and law seek to prevent by their laws of client confidentiality.

Doctors, lawyers and even pastors are not allowed to reveal or use information to manipulate or threaten clients. But that is exactly what the devil does. He claims to know God's servants in a way that people don't and he loves to use that power to intimidate and to destroy them if he can.

Nehemiah prayed to God to judge Sanballat and Tobiah for intimidating them.

"Hear, O our God; for we are despised: and turn their reproach upon their own head, and give them for a prey in the land of captivity:

And cover not their iniquity, and LET NOT THEIR SIN BE BLOTTED out from before thee: for they have provoked thee to anger before the builders" (Nehemiah 4:4-5).

9. Overcome the spirit of intimidation by living a righteous life.

Hereafter I will not talk much with you: for the prince of this world cometh, and hath nothing in me.
John 14:30

Jesus expected the devil to come to Him to tempt Him and to intimidate Him. That is for sure! Just as the night follows the day, you can expect demons to come your way saying, "I know you! I know about you! I know things people do not know!"

Have you never heard hate-filled rebellious people say, "I know him. You don't know him the way I do? I can tell you things that will make your jaw drop."

These people are mouthpieces of the devil, saying exactly what the demons said in the time of Jesus, "I know thee, who thou art!"

Jesus said that the devil could have no power or hold over Him. He was fearless in the face of the devil. Righteousness gives rise to a bold forthright ministry.

The wicked flee when no man pursueth: but the righteous are bold as a lion.

Proverbs 28:1

Through righteousness you can boldly face off the intimidations of the devil.

10. Overcome intimidation by praying for boldness.

Your life may not be as perfect as Jesus' was. But you can still be bold in the Lord and in the ministry. You need to pray for boldness to operate in the midst of alarming threats to your integrity and your ministry. God can give you boldness in spite of all your secret sins and the mistakes of your past.

PRAYING ALWAYS with all prayer and supplication in the Spirit, and watching thereunto with all perseverance and supplication for all saints; and for me, that utterance may be given unto me, THAT I MAY OPEN MY MOUTH BOLDLY, to make known the mystery of the gospel, for which I am an ambassador in bonds: THAT THEREIN I MAY SPEAK BOLDLY, as I ought to speak.

Ephesians 6:18-20

With all prayer and petition pray at all times in the Spirit, and with this in view, be on the alert with all perseverance and petition for all the saints, and PRAY on my behalf, that utterance may be given to me in the opening of my mouth, TO MAKE KNOWN WITH BOLDNESS the mystery of the gospel, for which I am an ambassador in chains; THAT IN PROCLAIMING IT I MAY SPEAK BOLDLY, AS I ought to speak."

Ephesians 6:18-20 (NASB)

Have you ever wondered why Paul prayed for boldness? You only sense a need for boldness when you are intimidated by something. Paul was surrounded by people who threatened to kill him if he continued to preach about Christ.

He was intimidated by the enemy and felt threatened. He felt like he was being asked to shut up or pay a high price. So he began to pray for boldness and God gave him the grace to continue his ministry in spite of the intimidations all around him.

Today, many of us lack the boldness to continue preaching the gospel of Jesus Christ. Many pastors are under pressure to preach about money, success and prosperity because that is what most people are preaching about.

The spirit of the world is so strong that pastors are intimidated when they preach the message of the pure gospel.

It is time to pray for boldness so that you can overcome the intimidation of the enemy.

The spirit of intimidation is a spirit that seeks to direct your life away from the will of God.

Stand up and keep going forward! You can make it! Do not be intimidated by the evil spirits that threaten you. God is granting you boldness and strength for the ministry that lies ahead of you.

CHAPTER 4

How Intimidation Can Stop You from Preaching

But even if you should suffer for the sake of righteousness, you are blessed. and do not fear their INTIMIDATION, and do not be troubled,

1 Peter 3:14, NASB

One day, I attended a very mournful funeral. As I stared tearfully at the person in the coffin, the Holy Spirit spoke to me and said, "This sadness is the result of man's rebellion." The Lord was not referring to that particular person but to death in general. "Rebellion is a very evil thing. Pride has caused men to rebel against God and this rebellion has resulted in the destruction of the human race."

Every funeral, every sickness, every death and every tragedy is ultimately caused by the rebellion and disloyalty of man to his maker. The Holy Spirit said to me, "Do not stop preaching about disloyalty. You are fighting a most terrible evil that plagues the human race. This evil will destroy the church if you allow it to flourish. Fight disloyalty, forgetfulness, and treachery with all your heart.

Don't allow it to take root!

Don't be intimidated by the rebellious enemies of this message!"

You see, on many occasions, attempts have been made to intimidate me from teaching on disloyalty. The whole Bible is a teaching on how man has been disloyal to God and the effects it has had on the human race.

Rebellious people dislike this message intensely. They have said many things on many occasions to make me feel bad about preaching about loyalty and disloyalty. There are many times I have felt like preaching about something else because of the intimidation that comes against the truth.

There are several examples of the spirit of intimidation rising up to stop you from preaching against disloyalty. Many of these things happened to me and therefore can happen to you.

1. Disloyal people will intimidate you by saying, "*He has no power in his ministry that is why he preaches about such things. He is just an administrator. He has no anointing and no 'spirit'.*" When I heard people commenting about my ministry like this, I was intimidated and I wanted to prove to

them that I had the anointing, I had the Spirit and I had power. I didn't want to be perceived as powerless as I preached my points on loyalty and disloyalty. But it is these very points on loyalty and faithfulness that have built and stabilized countless churches.

2. People may intimidate you by saying, "He has nothing to preach". One day after I finished preaching, an associate pastor told his senior pastor, "What is wrong with Bishop Dag? *Does he have nothing to preach about?* Who told him we are quarrelling in our church? Why does he keep on teaching about loyalty every time he comes here?"

3. I was intimidated one day when a pastor spoke about me and said, *"The message of loyalty and disloyalty is nonsense."* This fellow could not stand my preaching on the subject because he was just about to launch his breakaway church. On another occasion, a pastor jumped up and down on my book "Loyalty and Disloyalty". He wanted to smash it and pulverize it. He wanted to crush it into powder. *"It is nonsense, it is rubbish, it's a false doctrine,"* he shouted as he jumped up and down.

4. Disloyal people don't want you to speak about loyalty and disloyalty. It exposes them and makes everyone conscious of their activities. One day I was preaching about fathers and sons in the ministry. As I preached about how Absalom rose up against his father, someone shouted out, *"I am Absalom, eh...?"*

On another occasion, I taught on how Lucifer rebelled against God as he walked up and down in the midst of the stones of fire. Lucifer forgot that God had set him so, appointed him and made him who he was. This rebellious pastor reacted sharply and said, "O I see, I am now Lucifer? Are you now calling me Lucifer after I have served you for so long?"

5. Disloyal people like to make you feel like a bad and unloving father for correcting them or rejecting rebellious behaviour.

On different occasions I have had sons point me to Rick Joyner's book, *The Final Quest*.

One young pastor sent me a text and showed me the pages of the book, *The Final Quest*, that I should read. They were warning me by pointing out how bad spiritual fathers were judged in Heaven for rejecting their sons. Instead of correcting their proud and rebellious behaviour, they were intimidating me by accusing me of being a bad spiritual father. How wonderful! Someone even described my preaching as "a smear campaign".

When you hear these kinds of things, you can easily stop preaching about loyalty and disloyalty. You will fear for yourself and retreat from the conflict that comes from addressing disloyal and rebellious behaviour.

6. Disloyal people will try to intimidate you by saying that you run your church like a cult. A pastor whom I had appointed sent me a document that outlined the characteristics of a cult. He wanted me to change my message on loyalty and disloyalty, saying that it was something that cults taught.

   He said to me, *"It is not easy to leave a cult and it is not easy to leave your church. Because it is not easy to leave your church, your church may be a cult."* This fellow left my church, calling it a cult, but eventually came back to the "cult" after years of wandering about in the wilderness of ministry. You must not be intimidated by the truth of the Word of God, no matter what painful things people say about your message.

7. Disloyal people try to intimidate you by making you feel guilty and ungrateful. They try to make you feel that you are an ungrateful and an unreasonable person.

   One pastor said to me, "I have served you for five years."

   Another said, *"Is this what he is saying after I have built his system for him."*

59

Yet another said, *"Is this what he is saying after I have made him important for so many years?"* This chap called his service in the ministry: *"making Dag Heward-Mills important."* Obviously, he felt he was doing me a favour by being a minister in the denomination.

8.   Angry and disloyal people will try to intimidate you so that you do not say anything about them. A pastor's wife tried to calm her husband down as he ranted and raved about the church he was leaving. She said to him, "Don't say bad things about the church. Don't say bad things about the Bishop. Don't forget that you were trained and appointed by this very man of God."

But he would have none of that.

He said, *"I will be branded anyway. They will call me names when I leave; I know them."*

You see, this chap had been in the church for many years and knew all about rebellious behaviour. He himself had taught against disloyalty, but was now being disloyal in his moment of anger.

CHAPTER 5

Why You Should Not Be Intimidated

1. Do not be intimidated from preaching against disloyalty because you are fighting the spirit of death and desolation. The only thing rebellion has brought to this earth is death, sorrow, sadness and pain. Any fight against rebellion is a good fight and must be fought.

   ... and sin, when it is finished, bringeth forth death.
   James 1:15

2. Do not be intimidated from preaching against disloyalty because God's Word enjoins you to fight the good fight. Christianity involves fighting. Christianity involves waging war. We are to war a good warfare. You cannot and must not shy away from conflict if you want to be a good leader. People who shy away from legitimate conflict only live to have a worse problem on their hands later on.

   This command I entrust to you, Timothy, my son, in accordance with the prophecies previously made concerning you, that by them you may FIGHT THE GOOD FIGHT
   1 Timothy 1:18 (NASB)

3. Do not be intimidated from preaching against disloyalty because you must not lose even one of your sheep. Are you not a shepherd? Have you not got a divine mandate from God to look after the sheep in your care?

... those that thou gavest me I have kept, and none of them is lost...

John 17:12

Do not be intimidated because you cannot leave the sheep as prey for wolves. It is only hirelings who do not stand to fight for their sheep. "The hireling fleeth, because he is an hireling, and careth not for the sheep" (John 10:13). A good shepherd is a good fighter. A good shepherd is ready for conflict when it has to do with his sheep.

4. Do not be intimidated from preaching against disloyalty because you must not be deceived by the tricks and devices of the devil who comes as angel of light. Disloyal people come as angels of light. They come as men of good standing, impressive in the congregation. They use their gift to sway the simple and naïve ones amongst us. They lead away captive the young and immature sheep that God has entrusted in our care. It is your duty to confront these angels of light, no matter how polished, dignified or diplomatic they seem to be. You must tell them, "You are not an angel. I know you and I know what you are here for. You are a sheep thief! And I will fight with you for every single sheep in my care."

... such men are false apostles, deceitful workers, disguising themselves as apostles of Christ. And no wonder, for even Satan disguises himself as an angel of light.

2 Corinthians 11:13-14 (NASB)

Do not be deceived by these nice looking and nice sounding people. Many of them are so nice-looking and sounding that they could easily get jobs as television presenters or newsreaders. Such people are so nice that they are easily chosen to be school prefects, assistant school prefects and even presidents of countries (mind you, you need to look good and sound good to get any of these jobs).

5. Do not be intimidated from preaching against disloyalty because false prophets and teachers will abound in the last days. If you are not ready to confront false ministries that seek to divide and spread confusion you can never have a large ministry. You will know them by their fruit! When someone leaves confusion, destruction and division in his wake, the fruits speak for themselves.

When someone destroys what he has helped to build he makes his life a sinner according to the Bible. Why spend half of your life building something and the other half of your life destroying it? "For if I build again the things which I destroyed, I make myself a transgressor" (Galatians 2:18).

Paul teaches us to mark and avoid people who divide the flock and destroy the peace of the ministry.

Now I beseech you, brethren, MARK THEM WHICH CAUSE DIVISIONS and offences contrary to the doctrine which ye have learned; and avoid them.
Romans 16:17

How do you mark someone? You have to announce, teach and tell people about the dangerous activities of disloyal and rebellious persons! It is not a pleasant thing to mark people and to teach about them. But if you are not prepared to mark and avoid people, you cannot be a strong apostle and build many churches.

John Wesley, whose Methodist movement exists all over the world, was not liked by everyone. Not everyone liked John Wesley's leadership style. Not everyone liked John Wesley's teachings. But John Wesley told people that his church was not a democracy and that anyone was free to leave if they did not agree with him. You must be a strong leader. You must not be intimidated by those who naturally dislike authority and good leadership.

CHAPTER 6

Seven Things You Must Know about Confusion

1. CONFUSION IS THE LACK OF CLARITY. GOD IS NOT THE AUTHOR OF THINGS THAT ARE NOT CLEAR.

... let me never be put to confusion.

Psalms 71:1

Confusion results from a lack of clear and orderly behaviour. When someone is sometimes loyal and sometimes disloyal he is unclear about what he believes. God is not the author of things that are not clear or distinct. God is a God of light. Confusion is such a bad thing that David prayed that it should never happen to him.

2. CONFUSION IS A WEAPON OF WAR. SATAN LOVES TO CONFUSE THE LEADER AND MAKE HIM UNCERTAIN.

Let them be ashamed and confounded that seek after my soul: let them be turned backward, and put to confusion, that desire my hurt.

Psalms 70:2

When the leader is confused he is weakened and lacks the strength to advance with the needed force. The psalmist prayed that his enemies would experience confusion so that they would stop following him. The devil wants people to be confused and uncertain so that they can be turned back from pursuing him.

3. CONFUSION IS A WEAPON OF WAR. SATAN LOVES TO CONFUSE THE PEOPLE AROUND YOU.

Let them be confounded and put to shame that seek after my soul: let them be turned back and brought to confusion that devise my hurt.

Psalms 35:4

Satan loves to confuse the people so that they will have questions about you. Are you a good person? Are you a bad person? Are the stories we have heard about you true? Is there smoke without fire? Aren't you a thief as they said?

I tell you, it is difficult to have confused people in your congregation or in your leadership team.

There are always people who love you but who also distrust you. There are people who are both loyal and disloyal.

When in their company you never know what to preach about. You also never know whether to include them in certain meetings or not.

Satan prays continually that people who are after him should be confused. Satan is desperate because powerful anointed leaders are hounding him out of the communities and territories he has dominated for years. Satan does not know what to do to turn back the armies of the Lord so he throws darts and questions that set everyone thinking.

Soon, you have masses of confused people who are uncertain as to whether to turn left, right or go forwards or backwards.

4. CONFUSION IS DEMONIC! CONFUSION IS THE UNCERTAINTY, THE BLURRING OF THE LINES, THE MYSTIFICATION OF ISSUES, THE MIXING OF GOOD ATTITUDES AND BAD ATTITUDES.

Confused people are sometimes loyal and at the same time disloyal. Confusion is not from God. Confusion is from the devil. Confusion is a weapon of the devil.

For God is not the *author* of confusion, but of peace, as in all churches of the saints.

1 Corinthians 14:33

There are some people whose loyalty always comes into question. At times, the person may seem very loyal and at other times, disloyal.

Many people actually have this trait of being both loyal and disloyal. At times, they exhibit much loyalty and faithfulness and at other times, they are disloyal. Such people are confused.

It is important that you watch out for such people and note them carefully. They may be on your side or they may turn against you depending on the issue at hand.

I have such people around me and so does every leader. It is difficult to diagnose this mixture of loyalty and disloyalty. On more than one occasion, I have had people who named their children after me and hurt me at the same time. But they did me the great honour of naming their sons after me.

Years ago, I read from Kenneth Hagin about how someone had named her child after him. I thought to myself, "What an honour" but I never imagined that someone would do me such an honour one day. To my amazement several people have named their children after me. I see it as a great and permanent honour done to me.

But how could someone bestow on me such honour and hurt my ministry at the same time? One pastor named his son after me and within a few months, rebelled and took over the branch church he was pastoring. He renamed the church, led the congregation away and virtually stole our church.

All this was done shortly after doing me a great honour. I have experienced this kind of mixed loyalty more than once.

You may live with such people for years and never realize how they undermine you constantly, because they are also loyal to you.

I remember another member of my team who had supported the ministry for many years. I do not think I could have found a more loyal person whom I expected to be with me in ministry till the very end. His support was like the support of Joab, long-standing and unflinching.

And yet in this same character, I had a person who stirred up much dissension at meetings. On numerous occasions, his attitude stirred up discord amongst pastors, changed the course of happy fellowship times into sessions of debate,that left behind a very sour taste.

Over and over, he stirred up dispute in the name of being objective, frank and not being a "yes" man. He would often say that he was voicing the opinion of many who were simply not bold enough to bring out some of the issues. He did this with a good motive but the fruit of it was the disruption of pastoral meetings until I disliked having meetings with my own pastors.

Because of the permanent and unflinching loyalty of this same pastor, I was always confused and could not place my finger on what I was dealing with.

It was years after these experiences that I realized that I was dealing with a mixture of both loyalty and disloyalty in the same person. I know that the seeds that were sown at these meetings were not good things because of the fruit they bore.

What was the fruit of these "objective" discussions? The fruit of these debates was to turn the heart of the father away from the sons. Without knowing it, I lost interest in my own pastors and turned away from them. I disliked having meetings with my own pastors and unconsciously avoided them.

The Holy Spirit does not flow in an atmosphere of disputes. Disputes and debates stir up differences of opinion that divide the team. Once the unity and oneness is broken, the environment for the anointing is gone. Constant, rancorous debate may be good for parliament but it is not good for building an anointed team.

We are to preserve the unity of the Spirit in an atmosphere of peace. "Endeavouring to keep the unity of the Spirit in the bond of peace" (Ephesians 4:3).

Are there people in the Bible who are both loyal and disloyal? Yes. Joab is a good example of this mixture. His loyalty to David was long-standing. He supported David from the very beginning when David was not yet the king. Yet, Joab was a man who was both loyal and disloyal.

5. A CONFUSED PERSON WILL SUPPORT YOU AND OPPOSE YOU.

The Mixture of Support and Opposition

Joab is first mentioned when David was still a refugee in the wilderness being chased by Saul. Notice the loyalty of Joab and how it coexisted with disloyalty.

Notice how Joab supported David when he was not even in the ministry.

Joab supported David when he was still a refugee. There are friends that God gives you from childhood. Some of these people are faithful as you progress in ministry. Such people are lifelong supporters. "Then answered David and said to Ahimelech the Hittite, and to Abishai the son of Zeruiah, brother to Joab, saying,

Who will go down with me to Saul to the camp? And Abishai said, I will go down with thee" (1 Samuel 26:6).

Notice how Joab supported David when he was small and insignificant.

Joab supported David when he was a king of only one tribe. Anyone who supports you when you are nothing is real. Never let him go. He is one of the best things that ever happened to you.

People who love you when you are already successful must go further to prove that they really love you and not just the privileges of the rich and famous. "And Joab the son of Zeruiah, and the servants of David, went out, and met together by the pool of Gibeon: and they sat down, the one on the one side of the pool, and the other on the other side of the pool. And Abner said to Joab, Let the young men now arise, and play before us. And Joab said, Let them arise" (2 Samuel 2:13-14).

Notice how Joab fought many battles and engaged in many quarrels for David.

What a blessing it is to have someone who fights for you and takes some nasty blows on your behalf. Joab fought many wars on behalf of David. "And, Behold, the servants of David and Joab came from pursuing a troop, and brought in a great spoil with them..." (2 Samuel 3:22).

Notice how Joab eliminated rebels and other disloyal elements from the team.

Joab killed several people whose loyalties were questionable. He just could not stand people who were not totally committed to his king. He had an eye that saw these disloyal people whom people seemed to accommodate.

First of all he killed Abner who had supported Ishbosheth, the son of Saul for many years. "And when Abner was returned to Hebron, Joab took him aside in the gate to speak with him quietly, and smote him there under the fifth rib, that he died, for the blood of Asahel his brother" (2 Samuel 3:27).

Secondly, he killed Absalom, the son of David who overthrew his own father. "Then said Joab, I may not tarry thus with thee. And he took three darts in his hand, and thrust them through the heart of Absalom, while he was yet alive in the midst of the oak" (2 Samuel 18:14).

Thirdly, he killed Amasa who was appointed by Absalom as the commander of the armies that fought against King David. "But Amasa took no heed to the sword that was in Joab's hand: so he smote him therewith in the fifth rib, and shed out his bowels to the ground, and struck him not again; and he died" (2 Samuel 20:10).

Yet Joab opposed David when he chose Solomon to be the king. David chose Solomon to be the king but Joab supported Adonijah's attempt to be the king in place of Solomon. "Then Adonijah the son of Haggith exalted himself, saying, I will be king: and he prepared him chariots and horsemen, and fifty men to run before him. And he conferred with Joab the son of Zeruiah, and with Abiathar the priest: and they following Adonijah helped him" (1 Kings 1: 5, 7).

If you give somebody a name and people refuse to address the person by his new name, it is a demonstration of the people's rejection of your wishes, goodwill and authority.

It is surely a sign that reveals the heart of people. Also, if you give somebody a name and the person does not insist on being called by the new name, it reveals the extent to which your wishes and desires are accepted and supported by the person himself.

Dear leader, people will not tell you what is in their hearts because they cannot. Sometimes they do not even know what is in their own hearts. Watch out for people who do not support your wishes, desires and authority. Opposition exposes the hearts of people!

6. A CONFUSED PERSON WILL HONOUR YOU AND DISHONOUR YOU.

The Mixture of Honour and Dishonour

One of the things you must look out for is how people relate with those you have appointed. In a large church, this is the most revealing sign of disloyalty. In a large ministry people always have to deal with you through your representatives.

You get to learn about their real feelings towards you by observing how they relate with those you have appointed. Somebody who does not accept your wife does not accept you.

I always note people who are in constant dispute with my administrators, General Overseers, personal assistants and secretaries. To me, it is one of the clearest signs of disregard, disrespect and dislike for me personally.

You must understand how God feels when we criticize and reject the men He has called and anointed.

To criticize someone God has called and appointed is to say that God lacks intelligence and has foolishly appointed the wrong person. When people habitually fight and oppose those I have appointed, it sends a clear message to me!

Notice how Joab constantly recognized David's position and refused to take David's honour.

Joab called for David to come and receive the honour of the victories he had won in war. He did not take that honour for himself. Most assistants would like to take some honour for themselves.

A God-given loyal assistant is happy as long as his leader gets the credit. "And, Behold, the servants of David and Joab came from pursuing a troop, and brought in a great spoil with them..." (2 Samuel 3:22)

A mixture of loyalty and disloyalty is something most leaders are never able to deal with because they simply don't understand what they are dealing with.

Notice how Joab stayed with David to the very end. It is not easy to find people who will be with you all your life. That is the kind of person Joab was; he was there until the end. "Now the days of David drew nigh that he should die; and ... Joab" (1 Kings 2:1-5).

But right on the other hand, Joab dishonoured David by displacing and killing David's appointees. David appointed Amasa to be the commander of the army in place of Joab. "And king David sent to Zadok ...say ye to Amasa, Art thou not of my bone, and of my flesh? God do so to me, and more also, if thou be not captain of the host before me continually in the room of Joab" (2 Samuel 19:11-13). But Joab tricked Amasa and killed him when he was not expecting it. "But Amasa took no heed to the sword that was in Joab's hand: so he smote him therewith in the fifth rib, and shed out his bowels to the ground, and struck him not again; and he died" (2 Samuel 20:10).

7. A CONFUSED PERSON WILL OBEY YOU AND DISOBEY YOU.

A Mixture of Obedience and Disobedience

A loyal person is someone who will obey virtually every command. Joab's intense loyalty to David is shown by the way he killed Uriah, one of his own men, upon David's instructions. All he needed was a note from David and he would act on it. Joab obeyed every single instruction in David's letter. He needed no explanation in the note. David did not have to see Joab personally to explain how he had mistakenly impregnated Bathsheba. If David said to kill one of the commanders, then it would be done.

Indeed, there are not many people who are so obedient.

"And it came to pass in the morning, that David wrote a letter to Joab ... And he wrote in the letter, saying, SET YE URIAH IN THE FOREFRONT OF THE HOTTEST BATTLE, and retire ye from him, that he may be smitten, and die. And ... Joab ... assigned Uriah unto a place where he knew that valiant men were" (2 Samuel 11:14-16).

But right on the other hand, Joab killed people that King David loved. He did all these things against David's wishes.

Joab killed Abner in spite of King David's clear instruction on this matter. Abner had killed Joab's brother, Asahel and Joab had a personal score to settle with Abner.

Joab also killed Absalom even though David had clearly asked that Absalom should not be killed.

These actions clearly demonstrate the disobedience and disloyalty that was lurking within Joab. David never forgot the disloyalty of Joab, and on his deathbed, he instructed Solomon to execute Joab for these acts.

Perhaps David did not execute Joab himself because Joab had also been very loyal to him and fought many battles for him. "Moreover thou knowest also what Joab the son of Zeruiah did to me, and what he did to the two captains of the hosts of Israel, unto Abner the son of Ner, and unto Amasa the son of Jether, whom he slew, and shed the blood of war in peace, ...Do therefore according to thy wisdom, and let not his hoar head go down to the grave in peace" (1Kings 2:5-6).

CHAPTER 7

What is Familiarity?

Familiarity means to know someone or something so well and in such a way as to cause you to lose your admiration, respect and sense of awe.

David went home so he could ask the Lord to bless his family. But Saul's daughter Michal went out and started yelling at him. 'You were really great today!' she said. 'You acted like a dirty old man, dancing half-naked in front of your servants' slave girls.' David told her, 'The Lord didn't choose your father or anyone else in your family to be the leader of His people. The Lord chose me and I was celebrating in honour of him. I'll show you how great I can be! I'll even be disgusted to myself. But those slave girls you talked about will still honour me'. Michal never had any children.

2 Samuel 6:20-23
(Contemporary English Version)

1. Familiarity means to know someone or something so well and in such a way as to cause you to lose your admiration, respect and sense of awe.

Familiarity leads to presumption and arrogance. A person who suffers from familiarity becomes confident in a way that shows a lack of respect. Michal, the wife of King David, was so confident that she criticized the king for his style of praise and worship.

She knew the king so well as to lose her sense of awe. She criticized the king for his display of exuberance in front of girls she considered insignificant.

When people work closely with a man of God they tend to lose their sense of awe. Some also lose their admiration and respect. The loss of admiration and respect shows up in many subtle ways.

Michal, the classical critical and familiar wife, showed her lack of respect by the kind of remark or rebuke she made to her husband. Michal had become disconnected, critical and disloyal to her king. Michal had developed this attitude because she knew the king from head to toe. She had seen him playing with her like a little boy. She had related with him when he was in his most naked and unguarded moments.

This exposure had unfortunately eroded the mystification and awe that many held for the king. That is why she turned against him. This is what happens to many wives of men of God. There is nothing new under the sun. It is easy to become familiar and lose your sense of awe when you see a highly respected man sitting on the toilet or behaving like a gas bag in the home!

You need to have the gift of working in the king's palace to withstand the tendency to become familiar.

In the book of Daniel the three men, Shadrach, Meshach and Abednego were described as people who had the ability to work in the king's palace. There, they would see many private and uncomely things. They would see the base and human parts of the glorified royal family. Yet they would be required to maintain a genuine respect and awe for them. This is what is meant by having the ability to work in the king's palace.

"Children in whom was no blemish, but well favoured, and skilful in all wisdom, and cunning in knowledge, and understanding science, and such as HAD ABILITY IN THEM TO STAND IN THE KING'S PALACE, and whom they might teach the learning and the tongue of the Chaldeans" (Daniel 1:4).

2. **Familiarity afflicts the closest family and friends the most.** This causes anointed people to move away from their family and friends. Because of familiarity amongst those who you interact with closely, it is wise for ministers to constantly reach out to non-familiar groups.

These non-familiar groups may be people who are not your family or not close to you. Non-familiar groups are often the poor, the forgotten and the neglected ones.

3. **Familiarity has the power to neutralize the greatest of the gifts of God.** No matter how great the gift of God is, it can be neutralized by familiarity. Jesus was the greatest healer and teacher, yet his anointing was neutralized by the presence of familiar people!

Familiarity is the spiritual disease that can kill the ministry of a prophet. Familiarity was the most powerful antagonist to the anointing on Jesus' ministry!

Familiarity is the greatest block to the flow of God's power from God's servant!

And he went out from thence, and CAME INTO HIS OWN COUNTRY; and his disciples follow him. And when the sabbath day was come, he began to teach in the synagogue: and many hearing him were astonished, saying, From whence hath this man these things? and what wisdom is this which is given unto him, that even such mighty works are wrought by his hands? IS NOT

THIS THE CARPENTER, the son of Mary ... And they were offended at him. AND HE COULD THERE DO NO MIGHTY WORK, save that he laid his hands upon a few sick folk, and healed them.

Mark 6:1-3,5

4. **Familiarity is the cause of diminishing attendance at Christian programmes.**

Because ministers continue to minister in the familiar zones their impact gradually lessens until there is a perception that their season is past.

I once spoke with a minister who worked with a famous man of God. He was lamenting about the diminishing attendance at their crusades.

He described how he had had a crusade in a particular city and had a good attendance of twenty thousand people.

Then they had had a second crusade three years later and the attendance had dropped to twelve thousand.

Then they had a third crusade in the same city and in the same venue and this time the attendance was less than five thousand. This minister lamented because he felt the season for that man of God was over.

But I did not think so! I did not think his season was over. I remembered my own crusades. I remember having a very successful crusade with over ten thousand people in attendance. I was so encouraged by that crusade which was the largest crusade we had had at that time.

Because the crusade was so successful, I decided to have another crusade within twelve months in the same city.

To my amazement we struggled to have even six thousand people attend. That crusade became a turning point in my ministry. From then on I decided to avoid people who have become familiar with my ministry.

Have you ever wondered why Jesus moved away from His hometown Nazareth and went down to Capernaum, Chorazin and Bethsaida doing great miracles?

Jesus did not do great miracles everywhere. He did great miracles in particular places where they were not familiar with Him. Actually, most of His miracles were done in particular places. "Then began he to upbraid the cities WHEREIN MOST OF HIS MIGHTY WORKS WERE DONE, because they repented not" (Matthew 11:20).

5. Familiarity is the cause of spiritual barrenness.

Familiarity is the greatest block to receiving God's power. Because of familiarity, many people do not believe in the man of God. They do not believe the man of God has anything special to offer.

Because familiar people do not receive the power of God they do not amount to anything. They do not receive the teachings, they do not receive the revelations, they do not receive the blessings and therefore they remain in their barren state.

Great men of God are sent to them but they are unable to receive or understand anything that they say. Familiarity is one of the greatest causes of spiritual barrenness.

6. You can be close to a man of God without becoming familiar.

If you have the right attitude and the right heart you can be close to the power of God without becoming familiar.

There are many examples of people who were close to a man of God but did not become familiar. Many people actually use their privileged positions of closeness to receive the anointing.

Such people allow the strengths of their mentor to encourage them. But they also allow the weaknesses of their mentor to inspire them. They tell themselves, "If God can use a "normal" person like this man of God then He can use someone like me." They are simply not turned off by anything they see or hear. Three people stand out in this regard.

John was so close to Jesus that He entrusted His own mother to him. John described Jesus in a peculiar way in his famous epistle. John said, "The one who existed from the beginning is the one we have heard and seen. We saw him with our own eyes and touched him with our own hands. He is Jesus Christ, the Word of life.

This one who is life from God was shown to us, and we have seen him. And now we testify and announce to you that he is the one who is eternal life. He was with the Father, and then he was shown to us.

We are telling you about what we ourselves have actually seen and heard, so that you may have fellowship with us. And our fellowship is with the Father and with his Son, Jesus Christ." (1 John 1:1-3, NLT)

Somehow, John was not affected by having been so close to Jesus. He rather seemed overawed and full of faith that he had been with the Son of God Himself.

Mary and Martha were unaffected by their closeness to the Lord. Mary and Martha were blessed to have the Lord eating and resting in their home. Yet, they believed in His power to raise their dead brother, Lazarus, to life after four days.

"Then Martha, as soon as she heard that Jesus was coming, went and met him: but Mary sat still in the house. Then said Martha unto Jesus, Lord, if thou hadst been here, my brother had not died. But I know, that even now, whatsoever thou wilt ask of God, God will give it thee" (John 11:20-22).

It is encouraging to know that not everyone will fall to this deadly condition called familiarity. Leaders must search for people who have the ability to work closely without becoming familiar.

CHAPTER 8

Four Groups that Are Prone to Familiarity

L eaders must notice familiarity in the groups that are prone to it. Some people have a greater tendency to be familiar and presumptuous.

1. **People who frequently interact with the leader are prone to familiarity.**

   ... From whence hath this man these things? And what wisdom is this which is given unto him, that even such mighty works are wrought by his hands? Is not this the carpenter, the son of Mary, the brother of James, and Joses, and of Juda, and Simon? And are not his sisters here with us? And they were offended at him.

   Mark 6:2,3

2. **People who know too much about the leader are prone to familiarity.**

Where the people knew a lot about Jesus and His family, He was unable to perform miracles. They could only relate with Him as a carpenter. They had known Him as a brother of their friends. They had known Him as a son to Mary. They had known Him as an apprentice carpenter in Joseph's workshop. How could this man now claim to be the Son of God? It was preposterous. Yet Jesus was received in other towns where they were not familiar with His background. Today, Jesus is received all over the world with great faith and expectation because we do not have the problem of familiarity that His hometown had. This is why every leader should maintain a degree of mystique around him. The less people know about your private and uncomely realities and problems, the more they will be able to receive from you.

> And he could there do no mighty work, save that he laid his hands upon a few sick folk, and healed them.
>
> Mark 6:5

3. People who are friends of the leader are prone to familiarity.

Jesus' friendship with His disciples exposed the familiarity of Peter. One day, Jesus asked Peter for his opinion about His ministry. This question shows how Jesus was relaxed in the company of His disciples.

Unfortunately, Peter stepped out of line almost immediately and began to rebuke, correct and instruct Jesus on His future ministry plans. Close friends can step out of line when they take the privilege of closeness for granted.

> **He saith unto them, But whom say ye that I am? And Simon Peter answered and said, Thou art the Christ, the Son of the living God. And Jesus answered and said unto him, Blessed art thou, Simon Barjona: for flesh and blood hath not revealed it unto thee, but my Father which is in heaven.**
>
> **Matthew 16:15-17**

4. People who have been promoted are prone to familiarity.

Sometimes when people are elevated a little, they feel they are equal to their seniors and teachers. This is unfortunate.

Not everyone can handle promotion, elevation and blessings. Unfortunately, promotion corrupts and destroys many people. Upon graduation from the medical school we were given a certificate which reminded us not to become familiar. The first statement of the certificate read, "I shall show respect to my teachers..."

Peter was promoted and became the head of the church. He immediately began to step out of line, rebuking the Lord and forbidding Him to die on the cross.

He had a better plan for the salvation of this world. Peter rebuked God after his promotion. Perhaps that is why the Lord allowed him to be humiliated before the other disciples.

Peter's Appointment

And I say also unto thee, that thou art Peter, and upon this rock I will build my church; and the gates of hell shall not prevail against it.

Matthew 16:18

Peter Rebukes God after His Appointment

Then Peter took him, and began to rebuke him, saying, Be it far from thee, Lord: this shall not be unto thee.

But he turned, and said unto Peter, Get thee behind me, Satan: thou art an offence unto me: for thou savourest not the things that be of God, but those that be of men.

Matthew 16:22-23

CHAPTER 9

Twelve Signs of Familiarity

1. **Familiarity is shown when someone comments about things that are above him.**

   Then Peter took him, and began to rebuke him, saying, be it far from thee, Lord: this shall not be unto thee.

   Matthew 16:22

   The fact that your leader has discussed personal things with you does not mean that you should step out of order.

   One day, somebody made a remark about the type of food I ate at home. On another occasion, I heard a comment about the cat in my house. Yet on another occasion, I heard a comment about the food in my fridge.

   If an associate can comment about certain personal things without being asked to, it shows a certain level of familiarity.

2. **Familiarity is seen when someone finds faults with the leader and with his person.**

   Familiar people evaluate you in a carnal and natural way. Jesus was evaluated by the people in His town.

They scrutinized His family, His brothers, His sisters and His profession. Because the people of Nazareth were familiar with Jesus Christ and His family, they found fault with Him.

"From whence hath this man these things? And what wisdom is this which is given unto him, that even such mighty works are wrought by his hands? Is not this the carpenter, the son of Mary, the brother of James, and Joses, and of Juda, and Simon? And are not his sisters here with us? And they were offended at him" (Mark 6:2-3).

Jesus' own brothers did not believe in Him for obvious reasons. He was their very own brother. "For neither did his brethren believe in him" (John 7:5).

3. Familiarity is seen when someone attempts to correct his leader.

Then Peter took him, and began to rebuke him, saying, be it far from thee, Lord: this shall not be unto thee.
Matthew 16:22

Peter began to feel "extra free" after he was told "flesh and blood has not revealed this to you." He thought that he could now correct Jesus. Although every leader needs to be corrected, a subordinate is not qualified to do this.

4. Familiarity is displayed when someone attempts to direct and control his leader.

Then Peter took him, and began to rebuke him, saying, be it far from thee, Lord: this shall not be unto thee.
Matthew 16:22

Jesus was very quick to notice that Peter was out of order. Peter began to make pronouncements about the ministry of Jesus. Peter thought that his friendship with Christ gave him the authority to direct and to correct Jesus. Perhaps he thought that Jesus now wanted direction from him.

5. Familiarity is seen when someone uses privileges without asking for them anymore.

King David had a mule that was symbolic of his authority and power as a king. Anyone sitting on that mule was in charge of Israel. When David wanted to show the world that Solomon was the legitimate king, he asked that Solomon should be given the privilege of riding on his mule.

It may have been a little thing but it was enough to send the message to the entire city that Solomon was the legitimate heir to David.

Symbolic privileges are important because they help workers and associates to remember their true position. Anyone who casually presumes upon these privileges has become familiar.

The king also said unto them, take with you the servants of your lord, and cause Solomon my son to ride upon mine own mule, and bring him down to Gihon:

1 Kings 1:33

So Zadok the priest, and Nathan the prophet, and Benaiah the son of Jehoiada, and the Cherethites, and the Pelethites, went down, and caused Solomon to ride upon king David's mule, and brought him to Gihon.

And Zadok the priest took an horn of oil out of the tabernacle, and anointed Solomon. And they blew the trumpet; and all the people said, God save king Solomon.

And all the people came up after him, and the people piped with pipes, and rejoiced with great joy, so that the earth rent with the sound of them.

1 Kings 1:38-40

Whenever people trifle with the privileges of their leaders, they display a dangerous familiarity! The riding of David's mule was so symbolically powerful that everyone knew who the rightful king was.

Watch out for people who trifle with your symbolic privileges. They reveal a subtle, developing arrogance towards authority.

Sitting in My Chair

I once entered my office and found a junior pastor holding a meeting with some other pastors. He was sitting in my chair, behind my desk and everyone else was sitting around him.

He was conducting the meeting just as I usually did.

As soon as I saw him, I knew that something was wrong. Something was out of order. I immediately said to him, "Never sit on that chair again.

Never sit behind that desk again!" Then I told everyone, "If I am not here, no one should ever sit behind my desk or on my chair."

Indeed, over the next few years, this young man grew up to be proud and rebellious. His casual attitude toward my privileged position was a revelation of his deep-seated, pride-filled and rebellious nature.

6. **Familiarity is seen when someone uses privileges without saying thank you for them anymore.**

7. **Familiarity is seen when someone freely enters your room or office without knocking.**

8. **Familiarity is displayed when someone yawns and sleeps when you preach, teach or lecture.**

Preachers and teachers must watch out for yawning, especially when the yawns come at the beginning of the message.

Watch out for "early yawners"; they are usually suffering from familiarity. Such people feel that they know what you are going to say. They know you and they know what you usually say!

Truly, they have developed a familiar attitude towards your sermons, your CDs, your DVDs and your writings.

9. **Familiarity is exhibited when someone walks around, talks and chats whilst you are preaching.**

10. **Familiarity is revealed when someone is rude.**

The children of Israel had grown used to Moses even though he was such a great prophet. Korah openly challenged him, pointing out his faults. Only familiar people would dare to be rude to someone like Moses. This is the arrogance that develops with people who are too familiar with greatness.

And they gathered themselves together against Moses and against Aaron, and said unto them, Ye take too much upon you, seeing all the congregation are holy, every one of them, and the Lord is among them: wherefore then lift ye up yourselves above the congregation of the Lord?

Numbers 16:3

11. **Familiarity is displayed when someone is rude to people you delegate.**

And Moses sent to call Dathan and Abiram, the sons of Eliab: which said, we will not come up:

Numbers 16:12

Moses sent someone to call Dathan and Abiram. But they refused to come when Moses called them for a meeting. They said plainly: "We will not come." This kind of rudeness is what you find in presumptuous people suffering from familiarity.

There was no greater prophet than Moses. There was no prophet who had such teachings and writings. There was no prophet who had such signs and wonders.

And yet, there were people who were not afraid to be rude to him or to the people he had delegated. Indeed, some people are too familiar with greatness.

12. **Familiarity is demonstrated when someone raises his voice at you.**

CHAPTER 10

Seven Ways to Deal with Familiarity

1. **Address and confront all forms of familiarity urgently. Put subordinates who are out of order into their proper places.**

   But he turned, and said unto Peter, Get thee behind me, Satan: thou art an offence unto me: for thou savourest not the things that be of God, but those that be of men.

   Matthew 16:23

   Peter began to feel extra free. He became presumptuous and stepped out of order. He assumed he could correct Jesus. He thought his friendship with Christ gave him the authority to direct or correct Jesus.

   Peter thought his conversation with Jesus made him someone whose opinion had to be taken by Jesus.

   But Jesus quickly put him right. Jesus suddenly changed from a kind and gentle Jesus into a strong and tough Jesus. In a swift move, he cut Peter down to size.

   Why was Jesus transformed from a kind and gentle Jesus into a Jesus of steel? Why did He rebuke His close friend and associate in the harshest possible way? Why did He call Peter "Satan"?

Think about that! He needed to cut Peter down to size urgently. Jesus addressed and confronted familiarity with the utmost urgency.

2. **Avoid places where you are tolerated and go to places where you are celebrated.**

Avoid programmes in which the people have become familiar. Avoid places where the people take you for granted.

The Church that Tolerated Me

I once visited a church and ministered powerfully. After the service, I was seen off with the usual protocols. As I said goodbye to my hosts I sensed that I had been tolerated and not really appreciated. I was so sure of what I was feeling that I decided within me, whilst saying goodbye to my hosts that I would never go back there even if they invited me.

Jesus Christ set the example for overcoming familiarity. We see Him as He leaves familiar turf and heads for the non-familiar where little is known about Him.

There, He will be celebrated and many great miracles will take place. Read for yourself and see how Jesus recognized the deadly syndrome of familiarity and intentionally moved away from it.

Jesus Avoids Nazareth and Heads for Other Places

And he went out from thence, and came into his own country; and his disciples follow him.

And when the sabbath day was come, he began to teach in the synagogue: and many hearing him were astonished, saying, From whence hath this man these things? and what wisdom is this which is given unto him, that even such mighty works are wrought by his hands?

Is not this the carpenter, the son of Mary, the brother of James, and Joses, and of Juda, and Simon? and are not his sisters here with us? And they were offended at him.

But Jesus said unto them, A prophet is not without honour, but in his own country, and among his own kin, and in his own house.

And he could there do no mighty work, save that he laid his hands upon a few sick folk, and healed them.

And he marvelled because of their unbelief. AND HE WENT ROUND ABOUT THE VILLAGES, TEACHING.

Mark 6:1-6

3. Avoid familiarity by making clear distinctions between the different ranks of leaders.

Notice how Jesus sat on the donkey whilst the disciples walked. Jesus did not hire twelve donkeys so that they could all have donkeys. Notice how Jesus slept in the boat whilst the disciples rowed and worked hard.

Sometimes these differences are necessary to kill the spirit of familiarity. Do not feel shy to introduce necessary differences. It is these differences that may save your followers from familiarity.

4. Avoid monotony and repetitiveness in your ministry.

Introduce new ideas into your programmes. *Monotony incubates familiarity.* Don't always do what people are expecting you to do.

Repetitiveness, dullness and uniformity are the perfect contexts for familiarity. The same sermons in the same way from the same person at the same time have a way of incubating familiarity.

When the people wanted Jesus to come to their town to preach in the same old way, he refused to enter their monotonous pattern and decided to go to the next city.

He knew that they would soon be yawning at him whilst He preached. He knew they would soon be having discussions behind the stage whilst He ministered.

He knew people would be having little chats and jokes whilst he preached but suddenly sit up when His eye fell on them.

Jesus wisely decided to travel away to new territories.

It is good to have annual programmes but sometimes it is necessary to break monotonous patterns.

And when they had found him, they said unto him, All men seek for thee. And he said unto them, Let us go into the next towns, that I may preach there also: for therefore came I forth. And he preachedß in their synagogues throughout all Galilee, and cast out devils.
Mark 1:37-39

The very people who impress upon you to do what you have been doing all the time are those who become familiar.

It is because people know what you are going to do that they become familiar. Remember: too much knowledge incubates familiarity. Sometimes a prayer meeting or a worship session instead of the expected sermon will help to break the familiarity.

5. Teach about familiarity.

Ignorance is the breeding ground of demonic activity.

Teaching always serves to prevent the development of evil cankers in the ministry. Teaching is the greatest tool that prevents familiarity from developing in the ranks.

6. Teach against presumption.

Presumption is the arrogant assumption that privileges must be given to you. People who assume that they are entitled to certain privileges complain and murmur about things that are great privileges to other people.

Pampered and spoilt children complain about not having certain toys or games when many other children live in the desert hoping for a meal to keep them alive.

Equally, "spoilt" ministers complain about things which others would be grateful to have.

Tell people the value of the privileges they have. It is when people do not know the worth of something that they develop ungrateful and rebellious attitudes.

7. Teach people to have an attitude of thankfulness for everything.

You must teach people to be thankful on a minute-by-minute basis. This is what the Bible teaches.

You must teach people to be *thankful because it is a sign of the presence of the Holy Spirit.*

People who are filled with evil spirits are not thankful. People who are filled with evil spirits complain and murmur all the time. "And be not drunk with wine, wherein is excess; but BE FILLED WITH THE SPIRIT;

Speaking to yourselves in psalms and hymns and spiritual songs, singing and making melody in your heart to the Lord;

GIVING THANKS ALWAYS for all things unto God and the Father in the name of our Lord Jesus Christ;" (Ephesians 5:18-20)

[77]You must teach people to be thankful even in bad circumstances. "In every thing give thanks: for this is the will of God in Christ Jesus concerning you." (1 Thessalonians 5:18).